CONTENTS

Editorial, D. S. BELL and J. GAFFNEY — 1

The Gulf Crisis

Questions for the Future, EDGARD PISANI — 7

The Ambiguities of Justice: the Gulf War and the Future
of the Middle East, JAMES O'CONNELL — 14

What Future for European Security? ERIC REMACLE — 27

Justice and the Arab World, BUHRAM GHALIOUN — 47

Politics and International Law,
MONIQUE CHEMILLIER-GENDREAU — 63

The Ayatollah of the West, GÜNTHER NENNING — 75

The Gulf War: What Has Changed, ROBERT BISTOLFI — 81

The New International Order, GIANNI DE MICHELIS — 93

Lessons for After the War, PIERRE MAUROY — 100

Israel and the Gulf War, ELIE BARNAVI — 108

The Financial Consequences of the Gulf War,
PIERRE BÉRÉGOVOY — 115

French Intellectuals and Arab Nationalism,
RUDOLF EL KAREH — 124

The Twenty-first Century Has Arrived,
DIDIER MOTCHANE — 137

United Kingdom Defence Policy and the Gulf War,
JOLYON HOWORTH — 149

Document

Labour's Policy on the Gulf Crisis, MIKE GAPES — 165

Book Reviews

Edgar Morin and the New Beginning, SAMI NAÏR					177
    (Reviews of *Un nouveau commencement* by Edgar
    Morin, Gianluca Bocchi and Mauro Ceruti)
The Arab-Islamic World at the Crossroads of History,				181
    ETIENNE BUTZBACH
    (Reviews of *Laïcité ou islamisme, les Arabes à l'heure du*
    choix by Fouad Zakariya, and *The Arab World:*
    Nation State and Democracy by Fawzy Mansour)
The Three Cultures, GÉRARD DUPRAT						187
    (Review of *Die drei Kulturen* by Wolf Lepenies)

Editorial

The Gulf War may be behind us but the questions it raised as well as its consequences are not. This issue of *Contemporary European Affairs* is devoted almost entirely to the Gulf Crisis in its many aspects: political, economic, cultural, geo-strategic and, of course, moral. As the contributors are commenting on the unfolding situation, there is no 'Europe Now' section in this issue.

Edgard Pisani leads the discussion with a series of questions about the future, questions which arise from the Gulf Crisis itself, but which raise a complex series of questions related to the wider international order. Pierre Bérégovoy, the French Finance Minister, replies to a series of questions about the Gulf Crisis and, amongst other things, speculates upon the implications for North–South relations and for Europe. Mr Bérégovoy concludes by drawing attention to the need for European Community political unity in parallel with economic integration. The Italian foreign minister, Gianni De Michelis, also replies to a series of questions about the crisis, and in particular about the 'new international order'. De Michelis remarks that although Europe rose to the occasion by imposing sanctions on Iraq immediately after the invasion, maintained the coalition against Iraq, and helped countries inadvertently hit by the embargo, it was left behind by the military action. From this he concludes that Europe should move faster towards a closer political unity in the security, defence, and foreign policy realms, rather than accept the prevailing lack of European cooperation in the defence and foreign policy areas.

The leader of the French Socialist Party, Pierre Mauroy,

reviews the problems raised by attempts at a post-war settlement, and the difficulties in re-establishing some kind of equilibrium in the area. Pierre Mauroy, too, touches on the problems of Europe and also the North–South aspect to the crisis but his is a full exposition of the French Socialist Party's point of view on the evolving situation in its main aspects. This is followed by an article from Jolyon Howorth looking at the British position which was much more nuanced than was often portrayed (especially by a bellicose tabloid press). There is, he argues, a tension between the short term, tactical, considerations which the crisis evoked and the long-term, strategic objectives which remain. The solution to this dilemma involves a European commitment, and for the UK this—in the absence of Mrs Thatcher and the marginalization of most of the Tory anti-Europeanists—has become a possibility for the first time in a decade. Didier Motchane, a political theorist, and leader of the former CERES group in the French Socialist Party, as well as a member of the Directing Committee of the Party, writes about the difficulties which, as he sees it, arise from the Gulf Crisis. These problems include American leadership, continuing instability in the Middle East, and the need to rethink our attitudes to the state, to security, and to the nation in the light of this experience.

Eric Remacle looks at the impact the Gulf Crisis has had on European political unity, and at the United States' position in the Western Alliance. Remacle argues that the Gulf Crisis has served to give further power to American leadership, and that at the European level the war itself has led to a re-emphasis of the position of the nation state to the detriment of the integration process.

Buhran Ghalioun takes up the implications of the Gulf Crisis for the Euro-Arab dialogue. A new world order is, it seems, possible only if Europe can overcome its imperial legacy and outlook, and that means going beyond the destruction of the military powers of Iraq and the simple restoration of the status quo ante. Monique Chemillier-Gendreau, from the standpoint of a very personal vision of international law, argues that the United

Nations Charter was violated, manipulated, and ignored in the crisis leading up to the Gulf War. Elie Barnavi, on an optimistic note, writes about the Israeli position, and arrives at the conclusion that the present is an excellent time, one for peace making in the Middle East (assuming the window of opportunity is not lost). It was not, Professor Barnavi reminds us, Israel's war, but, politically, it became so, and as the crisis developed and the war progressed, the relationship between America and Israel became increasingly ambiguous. The key is to be found in the notion of linkage: not between the occupation of Kuwait and the Israeli–Palestinian conflict but between the ideas of a just settlement of the Kuwait–Iraq dispute and the Middle East problem as a whole. Rudolf El Kareh discusses the reaction of Western intellectuals who, for the most part, view the Arab world through a glass darkly; the debate, argues Professor El Kareh, has led to dangerous misinterpretations of this history of the Middle East (and to an abusive assimilation of Saddam Hussein and Hitler). There is here, argues Professor El Kareh, a complex reaction to the twenty year engagement with Islam by intellectuals of the West and a 'delegitimation' of Arab national-ism in general.

Robert Bistolfi takes a close look at the future of French relations with the region, with Israel, the Mediterranean, with the Arab world, and with North Africa. The crisis, he maintains, has revealed the limits of French ambition in the Middle East and has broken the link which once united France with the region. Professor O'Connell starts from the 'Just War' tradition of Western thought and asks whether the Gulf War falls into that category. His conclusion is that the war was not just and that an occasion was lost by President Bush to apply a policy of sanctions based on United Nations authority, a decision which will have long-term implications. Günther Nenning replies to Hans Magnus Enzensberger's view that the War was a just War, published in *Die Zeit* and which had widespread ramifications. In Germany, unlike Britain there was a basic reluctance to believe that war was necessary (or, indeed, that peace would not be preserved). The dossier on the Gulf comprises a series of texts.

These are brought together and commented on by Mike Gapes from the perspective of the British Labour Party's response to the Gulf Crisis. The Labour Party, probably nervous of its 1987 election mauling—widely imputed to the then defence policy—adopted a 'tough but patient stance' and avoided being caught too far left of the Conservative government.

The Book Reviews in this issue cover some of the same ground. The first is a review of Edgar Morin, Gianluca Bocchi and Mauro Ceruti's *Un nouveau commencement* in which they speculate about the post modern world. The second is Etienne Butzbach's review of the struggle within Islam, *Laïcité ou islamisme, l'heure du choix* which is a series of articles by Fouad Zakaria first published in Cairo and which is a hard look at the intellectual Arab world. Also covered in this review is Fawzy Mansour's *The Arab World: Nation, State and Democracy* (also first published in Cairo). These three books form a unilateral and historical contribution to the continuing debate. The last review by Gerard Duprat is of Wolf Lepenies *Die drei Kulturen* which analyses the rise of sociology as a discipline in France, Germany, and the United Kingdom.

D. S. Bell and John Gaffney

The Gulf Crisis

Questions for the Future

Edgard Pisani

1. Is there such a thing as Arab unity? Has it been destroyed? Can it be rebuilt? If not, towards which organizations will the Arab world turn to guarantee its future? Are not the myths in all this more potent than the realities?

2. The European Community played no role in the conflict. Does it see this problem as an insurmountable one or, encouraged by its own setbacks, as it were, will it try to equip itself with the politico-strategic capacity that will make it into a great power? How will it do this? Will it be so concerned about Eastern and Western Europe that it forgets the poorer countries of the Southern hemisphere?

3. Does the silent, submissive Soviet Union which was the objective accomplice of the Anglo-American initiatives during the conflict, still have the ability, over and above its media initiatives and self-publicity, to play a major role in the Near and Middle East? Could it conceivably abandon its role? And if it were to, could it ever regain it?

4. The United States became massively engaged in the conflict both in the diplomatic phase before the war as in the war itself, and, indeed, in the post-war diplomacy. Did they do this to guarantee and uphold the international order, to guarantee the world's oil production, to protect the state of Israel, or as a great

7

power bent on controlling, for its own gain, a strategic region of the world?

5. Has Israel now come to realize that it is time to abandon the defensive–aggressive stance it has developed for its own survival and expansion, and is it ready to see that the recent upheaval is a unique opportunity to define a regional balance and security in which it has its own place, first in a truce and later in co-operation with the Arab world that surrounds it?

6. Has Iraq, which has been crushed by a hi-tech war, retained the capacity in human and physical resources and political dynamism to survive the war, the dictatorship and the new war? Can it ever find a way of playing a regional role that is acceptable to its neighbours? Will the coalition realize that Iraq is necessary to the stability of the region? Can the Iraqi people, mistreated, oppressed, and wounded, find their voice once again and their cultural richness and creativity?

7. Does Iran hope to profit from the disorder in the region, and take revenge for the humiliating defeat it suffered at the hands of Iraq? Or will it agree to participate in regional stability, or try to gain new advantages? Has it abandoned its ambitions concerning the spread of a fundamentalism that knows no frontiers?

8. Will Turkey, the declared ally of the USA and NATO's outpost, guardian of the memory of the Ottoman Empire, and an Islamic country in the process of modernization, and neighbour of the Soviet Union, seek peace or does it see itself as one day, once again, a great power?

9. Does President Hafez al Assad of Syria who, with a small minority governs skillfully and firmly a country with a long tradition, intend to annex Lebanon, via the old links with the Baath party. Does he envisage Syria and Iraq as a single state? Does he, using his consummate skill, want to dominate an

organization which, including Egypt, Saudi Arabia, and the Emirates, would have great strategic power? Is not the coalition that has been sketched out in Damascus the negation of what is needed for regional stability?

10. After having welcomed the 'infidel' armies, will Saudi Arabia find again the dual role it had played as both a kingdom and the country responsible for the holy places? Will it continue along the road to social modernization that the war may have encouraged? Will it continue to believe that with its strong religious authority, and all its money, it has a decisive role to play as the partner of the USA, and at the same time as the propagator of Islam? Will it see itself as a secular regional power in search of stability or as an international religious power? Are the two roles compatible?

11. Will Egypt, who played a decisive role in the early weeks in August 1990 and until now has drawn immense financial profit from the war, now consider that the time has come to build an economy commensurate with its needs and the expertise of its population? Or does it intend to play a leading role in terms of the Camp David agreements and its allegiance to the USA? Will it be able to arbitrate between its role as a leading Arab country and that of privileged interlocutor of the US?

12. Will Lebanon feel that a new peace dominated by Syria will give it the possibility of rebuilding its pluralist democracy, and give back to Beirut its former role? Or does it wish to partake of the continuing contest between the warring clans, a scenario that will deprive it of any hope for future autonomy? Will the international community feel that Lebanon's independence and international integrity will be a necessary prerequisite to regional stability?

13. Will the Yemen, which has perpetually taken the risk of irritating its vast and rich, though sparsely populated, neighbour, continue to play an independent role, or will it simply follow

the post-war logic of trying to draw maximum profit from the situation?

14. Will Kuwait take the opportunity of renewing and extending its democratic tradition, or will the Emir and his family seek revenge for their misfortune by setting up a royal political family with strict control of the country's resources? Rich in oil and overseas capital, will it, after having rebuilt the country, be the skillful financial operator that will help correct the instability of the whole region? Will it find a way of reconciling the needs of the region's population with the riches that lie under the ground? Will Kuwait manage its oil production in such a way as to control the fluctuations of world oil prices as to benefit both producers and consumers?

15. Will there be a solution to the problem of the Kurds, a solution which fulfills the aspirations of self-identity without destabilizing the whole region?

16. After its inevitable commitment to Saddam Hussein, will the PLO come up with, while remaining true to itself, realistic political proposals that will facilitate the birth of Palestine? Will Arafat realize that the chance he well deserves to accomplish the task he has undertaken exists *both* in the *Intifada* and in the putting forward of proposals which will get Israel–Arab discussions going again? And will the US finally see that the existence of Palestine is necessary to the stability of the region?

17. Will the North African countries give substance to their unity by enhancing their economic policies and developing their economies in co-operation with their near-neighbour the European Community? Committed to different though converging democratic processes, will the countries of North Africa be able to resist the wave of populist Islam?

18. Is the claimed return to true Islamic origins in the Arab world a denial of modernity and a turning in on oneself or is it, rather, a moment of recuperation before the Arab world embarks upon new roads of controllable modernization which will allow for a new cultural enrichment?

19. Why have Morocco, Tunisia, and Algeria, the most secular countries and the most committed to the democratic process in the region, been those who gave the most verbal support to Saddam Hussein's adventurism?

20. Will the Arabs in the contexts of Islam, tradition, change, and growth be capable of investing the rules and democratic structures which will respond to the hopes that are expressed within the Arab community?

21. Will the Arabs divide up—following the orientations during the Gulf war—between members and non-members of the coalition, with the US co-operating with the former and ignoring the latter? Will the structures that will be put in place be long lasting or will we see for the foreseeable future an Arab council chaired by an American Secretary of State?

22. Will the USA be able to leave the Middle East after having dominated, pacified, and organized the whole situation, or will they try to hold on to something? Will they be able to accept that thanks to the dialogue between Europe and some of the Arab countries a truly Mediterranean region is developing, a region that will be the guarantor of a truly multi-cultural exchange between the North and South?

23. Will the United Nations have the strength to undertake a thorough evaluation of the conditions in which they were involved in the Middle East? Will we be able to say that in fact the United Nations' Charter was not totally respected over this whole issue. Can the UN define with greater precision future conditions of involvement of troops going into action under the auspices and with the authorization of the UN?

24. Will the New International Order which is, after all, nothing more than the proper application of the UN Charter, comply with all the resolutions in the Security Council which to date have not been applied? Will such compliance, moreover, imply military interventions even if they are not on the scale of the Gulf War? Will what happened in the Gulf be the exception or the rule in terms of future developments?

25. Will the New International Order express itself only at the level of security, and only as a rectification of transgressions, or will it undertake a permanent effort to alleviate tensions whatever their nature? Will the New International Order become the means whereby a New International Economic Order is found which will be capable of confronting the problems posed by the co-existence of two huge groupings, the one rich and in demographic decline, the other expanding rapidly demographically and yet held in poverty?

*   *   *

These questions in fact point us towards the future alternatives open to us:
● was the Gulf war necessary for the creation of stability in the Middle East, or was it a demonstration of force whose only objective was to secure for the rich countries the oil they need?
● is the New International Order one which does not tolerate abuse, and will the resolutions of the Security Council, past, present, and future, therefore, all be applied, and ultimately backed up by resorting to force if necessary, or else is the New International Order just the façade of a circumstantial undertaking which was dictated by particular interests?
● is the New International order now restrcted to activity that is controlled by the UN, or it is also part of the Bretton Woods agreements, the World Bank, the IMF, and the UN agencies involved with a development council whose task is to create the discipline and the rules of a fair and durable management of the

world's resources and one which will benefit everyone and respect the environment?

● will a responsible international order related to the whole international community strengthen international law based upon the UN Charter, or will the New International Order be the juridical apparatus used by one power, and its allies, and who assumes that it alone has the right to organize the world according to its own view and its own interests? International law must be universal, and defined by all those who it will apply to, or it will be merely an abuse of law itself.

The Ambiguities of Justice: the Gulf War and the Future of the Middle East

*James O'Connell**

In this article I begin by sketching the principles of a just war. Though I will refer to them only occasionally I want to keep them in mind throughout the discussion. Then at the end I will return to them explicitly. The bulk of the paper seeks to describe, analyse and reflect on Middle Eastern politics and the effect that the Coalition intervention will have in the area. Only in this way can one make a moral judgment on the war and take a stand with personal integrity.

The interplay of the conditions for a just war

The condition of a just war that is usually the most immediately considered by those involved in deciding whether or not to go to war is that the cause for which it is fought be just. In modern times philosophers and theologians have interpreted this condition in terms of defence against unjust aggression. In the case of the war to liberate Kuwait the cause is manifestly just: not only should a small state not be swallowed up by a larger neighbour but it should also not fall under the control of a cruel despot.

There are however other conditions besides just defence that need to be taken into consideration in opting for war. One

* Professor of Peace Studies, University of Bradford, UK.

14

condition (proportionality) seeks to balance in a practical judgment the foreseeable costs of a war against its gains. Another condition, based on our common humanity, insists that acts of war should not be directed against non-combatants (discrimination). There is also a condition that war, because of its evils, be undertaken only as a last resort. In spite of the relevance, and often the strength, of the other conditions for a just war, those who oppose a war—or who at least hang back from supporting a war—that has a just cause find themselves faced with some embarrassment since the condition of defence against aggression is psychologically the most salient and morally the most legitimizing condition of just war for most persons. Given these considerations, the Gulf war has provided no small embarrassment for many thoughtful commentators who have refused to endorse the war. For that reason—among others—I will try in this article to suggest the interrelationship of the factors involved in reaching a decision on going into this particular war.

It is difficult—to begin with—not to sigh for a 'might have been' and lament the judgment that led President Bush in the face of a gross violation of international law and the perceived threat to Western access to oil at reasonable prices to have precipitate recourse to military measures: he chose to send, shortly after the invasion of Kuwait, huge rather than token forces into Saudi Arabia; and once he had done that, he had then in the face of problems of military logistics and morale little option except to use those forces in going to war. In consequence, an opportunity for making sanctions work that might have provided a most salutary contemporary precedent was lost, even if it is acknowledged that sanctions were likely to take a long time; and an opportunity was also missed for creating a new international atmosphere in which war options were taken up more slowly and more reluctantly than in the past. In short, President Bush not so much went to war too soon but with the connivance of his adversary, President Saddam Hussein, who refused to negotiate seriously in the days before the war began, he made war well-nigh unavoidable too soon. Yet if President Bush failed to exhaust other reasonable means, particularly sanctions, before going to war, once the war had become inevitable or had actually got under way, those who needed to take a stand had then to do so in the light of the other moral and political considerations of the just war theory.*

Freeing Kuwait: simple purpose and complex circumstances

There is a barren simplicity and a dreadful complexity to war and peace in the Gulf. Peace can return now that Iraq has been driven out of Kuwait. Some members of the Coalition, the Soviet Union, and various other countries have however made clear that they will not support—unless Saddam Hussein's intransigence and the military situation leave them no alternative—broadening the initial UN aims into destroying the Iraqi regime. Yet the Americans and the British have made clear informally that they see the removal of the Iraqi President as one of the aims of the war. After the cease-fire the question is what efforts and resources will be put into rebuilding Iraq and Kuwait. But once peace comes in the complex wake of a war that has changed the patterns of Arab alliances, that has dramatized cleavages between Muslim peoples and their governments, that has created new social awakening among peoples deprived of democracy and human rights, that has questioned anew the nature of the American and European presence in the Middle East, and that has provoked once more the ruthlessness and intransigence of Israeli fear and ambition, such peace will not be the same as the peace that preceded the war.

Though whatever peace is to be made will be conditioned by

---

*I found British support for the war—which far outdistanced that of the other members of the European Community, most of whom went along only reluctantly with it—peculiarly painful. It seems to me that it is in good measure based on a desire to put together again a tattered special relationship with the United States which had come apart as the Americans recognized that real power in Europe had come to lie with the Germans, as the British had put themselves in the wrong in being opposed to or being lukewarm about German unity, and as the Americans supported moves towards further European unity that the British were reluctant to accept.

the shape of the war's ending. If Saddam Hussein's regime is ousted, the eventual outcome of the war may prove relatively straightforward. Though there has been talk of reparations being extracted from Iraq to compensate Kuwait, the latter country has more than enough financial capacity of its own, allowing for some immediate outside help to facilitate cash flow problems, to repair the material damage inflicted on its territory. Moreover, a bankrupt Iraq with a great part of the modern sector of its economy in ruins is in no position to pay reparations. The American government has so far accepted this conclusion in that it has talked about its own participation in re-building Iraq after the overthrow of Saddam Hussein. If the present regime survives, the Americans and the British will undoubtedly initiate discussion about war crimes and make token demands for reparations. They will especially refuse to take part in rebuilding Iraq and hope to provoke reaction against a regime that would in any case face enormous problems in the wake of a lost war into which it has with such disastrous judgment and wicked folly led its people. Finally, since the Americans and the British have made known that they may keep some sea and air forces in the Gulf ('over the horizon' forces) but will not keep land forces, a scheme to provide such forces is already taking shape in the form of an Egyptian army presence (and possibly Syrian as well) in return for a substantial payment from the Gulf states, especially Saudi Arabia, and investment help.

Yet simple as the shape of the peace may be, it is much less clear who is going to impose or make the peace. Those who are taking a military part in the Coalition believe that they have a right to share the decisions of the settlement. Yet a crucial actor, Iran, which has remained neutral and which is not an Arab state has, in undertaking mediation efforts and in stressing its pivotal role in the Middle East, been reserving a place for itself; and in any case it is manifestly impossible to leave Iran out of a settlement since it is the most populous and potentially the most powerful military state in the Gulf. Moreover, the Soviets, through their ingenious and patient brokerage, have made a strong case for a role in the peace of a region with which it shares frontiers and concerns. The Americans and the British may find that once a peace conference—which must be distinct from a longer term settlement process in the Middle East—is convened Arab and Islamic alliances, that are bent on protecting their own immediate interests in the region and more interested in future power and economic relations with one another than in weakening Iraq, may take over political control of the conference and marginalize the military victors. Moreover, the legitimacy of the victors has suffered damage from the growing uneasiness and dismay with which the Soviet Union and other countries, including India and many Third World countries, have reacted as American bombing has almost obliterated the modern sector of the Iraqi economy and inflicted heavy casualties on the population as well as on Iraqi conscripts and reservists. In the event, the Americans may find, for example, that their influence at the conference may much more depend on the financial resources that they are willing to put into the region and the resources that they can cajole for reconstruction out of rich allies such as Saudi Arabia than on their military capability and prowess during and after the war.* In short, it is far from clear that those who won the war will shape the peace.

Elements of a settlement

It may be worth while to pick out elements of an immediate peace settlement in the aftermath of the war. These elements are.

1. the establishment of an arms control and verification system (particularly in respect of long range ballistic missiles, chemical and bacteriological weapons, and nuclear and near nuclear

---

* In the period leading up to the war various conciliatory proposals were put forward that, in return for an Iraqi withdrawal from Kuwait, offered Iraq the two islands it claimed in the Gulf as well as the disputed oilfield on the Iraqi–Kuwaiti border. The victors in the war are most unlikely to make such concessions. Yet, particularly if the Iraqi regime changed, there may be a case for Kuwait to make negotiated concessions to consolidate the peace in offering some gains to a devastated Iraq. However, I realise how difficult it would be for many to accept such proposals.

capacities), initially in the case of Iraq but accepted as extendable to other countries;

2. control over arms sales and exports, including those to Israel, to moderate military competition in the region;

3. acceptance of outside military forces for a time to provide security guarantees to various Gulf states—with the intention of turning such presence into a UN presence;

4. acceptance in principle of security for Israel, autonomy for a Palestinian state, and measures that go some way towards meeting Kurdish aspirations;

5. a commitment to rebuilding the Iraqi and Kuwaiti economies;

6. an undertaking to spread resources more evenly between the oil rich states and the more populated and poorer states of the region.

The shadow of long term complexity and disequilibrium

The very simplicity of the peace objectives constantly enunciated by President Bush and other Coalition leaders suggests the short range of the means used to free Kuwait. Kuwait may have been freed; Iraq may have been economically ruined and militarily defeated; but none of the main and long term problems of the Middle East have been more than begun to be resolved. However the peace conditions mentioned in the previous section as being required to accompany the objective of the war adumbrate those larger problems that bedevil the region. What are these problems?

First, the Gulf emirates still seek to possess military forces that are equipped with modern armaments for which they cannot find the skilled personnel required to deploy them;* their

---

* Mohamed Sid-Ahmed points out perceptively in *The Guardian* (5/2/91): 'The cohabitation of rich oil states with sparse populations, no accountable institutions and sophisticated military hardware without the personnel to man them, side by side with densely populated states, unable to cope with the burden of inextricable economic difficulties and with developed, experienced armies, was conceivable as long as bi-polarity worldwide was transposed into the Arab world and as long as the cold war could immunise the oil-rich states against the threat of "revolutionary" regimes.'

governments remain in the hands of privileged minorities that
are vulnerable to internal and external destabilization; vast hordes
of guest workers are likely to be less quiescent in the future than
in the past; and the immense oil revenues will go on provoking
resentment and envy.

Second, an embarrassing political weakness in the position of
the small and rich Gulf states is that they depend heavily on
Western patrons who come from outside the region, who are
linked with a colonial past, who have in measure been enemies
from the time of the Crusaders, and who are the current
possessors of global economic privilege. In this new situation it
is impossible for Western powers to play for long the role of
either policeman or bouncer—the failure of the American
move into Lebanon under President Reagan made this
clear.

Third, Egypt, Iraq, Turkey, and Iran face enormous difficulties
of development that may lead them into the hands of radical
oppositions or provoke moderate governments into radical
posturing.* The Jordanian regime may fall in the wake of the
war and its economic hardships. Iraq, Turkey, and Iran have to
face a resurgent Kurdish nationalism and rebellions.

Fourth, countries as far apart as Algeria, Morocco, and Turkey
as well as other countries in the Arab and Muslim world may
face new mass movements that find support in conservative
Islamic reactions and create opportunities for populist leaders
who reject a Western presence in their region, and who may try
to impose backward looking conditions on their elites and
peoples.

* The difficulties confronting Egypt and Turkey from population growth
alone may be seen from noticing the extraordinarily rapid demographic
growth in each country and by comparing them with Italy and France. Italy's
population, for example, in 1950 was 47m, while Egypt's was 20m. Italy's
population is forecast to be 59m in the year 2000 and Egypt's 63m. France's
population in 1950 was 41m, while Turkey's was 21m. France's population is
forecast to be 57m in the year 2000 and Turkey's 65m. The Mediterranean
figures and forecasts are discussed meticulously by Luigi di Comite and
Maria Rosaria Carli, 'Demographic Development in the Mediterranean area',
Mediterranean Social Sciences Network, No. 4 (1990).

Fifth, Israel appears to remain obdurate in its refusal to negotiate with Palestinians, refusing to trade territory for security and peace, confounded by a continuing *intifada*, harassing and exploiting the people of the Occupied Territories, tempted to find excuses to expel Palestinian leaders and populations, surreptitiously sending more Jewish settlers into the West Bank, wrapping its attitudes in a sense of siege, and refusing to accept that the advent of ballistic missiles in the Middle East has changed traditional military forms of security.*

Sixth, while Israel defies the Arab and Muslim world and stays immobile in its foreign and regional policy, Syria which is receiving funding from Saudi Arabia and which is buying new arms from China and North Korea for its substantial military forces is consolidating its presence in Lebanon and waiting for destabilization in Jordan to intervene opportunistically so as to create eventually the Greater Syria of its aspirations. Though these aspirations are almost certainly futile, they could lure Syria still further into the Lebanese morass, add to the myriad complications of the bitter divisions in that country, and lead to trouble in Jordan as well. Syria also festers in bitterness over the Israeli occupation of the Golan Heights and envisages much of its military build-up in terms of a possible confrontation with Israel. Israel in the wake of the norms that have been elaborated to justify the Gulf war may find it possible to deter a Syrian military attack but may find it much more difficult to counter Syrian interventionism in Jordan and Lebanon and to block Syrian expansionism.

Seventh, the Kurdish issue remains unresolved. Though as a people they are mentioned as early as the sixth century BC in Assyrian records, divided between Turkey, Iraq, Syria, and Iran the Kurds have made no proper advance towards statehood. In spite of earlier promises they eventually lost out in the colonial divisions carried out by France and Britain in the aftermath of

---

* Israeli social and economic structures are also being weighed down with immense burdens as Soviet Jewish immigrants pour into a country that is presently ill-prepared to receive such numbers.

World War I and have never even been able to profit much
from the disputes between their occupying powers. Iraq even
authorized Turkey in 1983 to attack the Kurds within Iraqi
frontiers; and then towards the end of its war with Iran Iraq
used chemical weapons against Kurdish villages. Whether it is a
question of establishing a state or autonomous regions, few
peoples have a case for national recognition as much as the
Kurds; few peoples also have fought so hard during this century
to assert themselves; and few have had their human rights
violated with such systematic repression and cruelty.

Eighth, an enduring and unresolved set of conflicts over the
use of water resources pervades the Middle East. Iraq, Turkey,
and Syria have been time and again in dispute over the Tigris
and the Euphrates. More acutely again, Israel worries over water
resources, seeks in practice to make the Litani river in the south
of Lebanon its frontier, and draws disproportionately on the
wells and underground water of the West Bank—and yet like
Jordan it is faced with outrunning its existing water reserves
within fifteen years, if not sooner. Israel may be more willing to
give up land than water. Sensible management of Middle Eastern
water supplies will require agreement and cooperation among a
number of countries that live at the moment in malign tension
with one another.

Given the complexity of this overall situation, several considerations need to be kept in mind. First, the United States is
in no position of political knowledge or financial capacity to
play a Middle Eastern policing role, much less a global role.
Nonetheless the United States could play a useful broker's role
in the Middle East by persuading Israel to take a less intransigent
stand on the Palestinian issue, by using its influence with the
emirates to persuade them to invest in the region, by itself
supplying more non-military aid, and by undertaking sensible
negotiations with Iran and Iraq to ensure future stability. Second,
were some equivalent of the Kuwaiti invasion to recur, there is
little possibility of reassembling for reasons of political will or
financial capacity a vast armada on the scale of Operation Desert

Storm.* In other words, the future limitations of American power should be kept in mind to mitigate the temptation to believe that an American–Soviet bi-polar military world has been replaced by a uni-polar world headed by the United States. The United States may be the most powerful state in the world. That does not mean that it can easily wield its military power in what is a new multi-polar political situation or that it can impose its hegemony on every other state in a uni-polar military system as well as on the whole network of international politics. Iraq's present defiance—as Iran's at an earlier stage—illustrates those American limitations. Third, Western countries generally are likely to want to play no more than an economic and mostly trading role in the region.† Fourth, there is a vital need to rethink and to rework existing Arab international bodies as well as to create regional structures in the Middle East within which the states and peoples belonging to the area‡ can sort out their political problems, coordinate investment and industrial policies, and seek to deal collectively with outside countries that have an interest in ensuring the maintenance of oil and other trade with the region. Finally, Arab groups generally will do well to advert to the lack of developed human rights in their countries and to move towards more democratic structures in order to cope with

* There is a strange irony about the role of the Cold War in the present dispute. The United States from its hostile relationship with the Soviet Union was led to accumulate the galaxy of forces and the arsenal of modern weapons that are being used in the Gulf. But it is the unfreezing of American and Soviet hostility that has enabled the United States to transfer its military effort to the Gulf and leave Central and Western Europe without forces and equipment that were thought for some forty years to be vital to its defence. Moreover, in the context of the end of the Cold War and the Soviet Union's economic and ethnic problems, Saddam Hussein misunderstood the changed international situation and failed to understand that old rivals would collaborate in cutting him down to size.

† There are roles open to European countries that are consonant with their political and economic power and interests. Again one must envisage brokerage roles; and these roles are meant mostly to help local groups to develop economically and to reach inter-state political, economic, and security agreements where they cannot readily do so on their own.

‡ There is also a case for collaboration between Middle Eastern regional institutions and those of the Arab North African countries.

deficiencies that in good part underlie Arab backwardness and despotism.

Reflections in the guise of a conclusion

Putting together reflections that draw on the descriptions and analysis of the previous paragraph, one may suggest that the United Nations resolutions and Coalition declarations had four objectives: restoring the sovereignty of Kuwait; deterring future aggressors; establishing a new stability in the Middle East; and moving to create a new world order. I want to suggest that none of these objectives is likely to be fully achieved: not even Kuwait will emerge as before and its ruling groups are unlikely to recover from the interregnum of occupation; those with grievances or fears are likely to go on preparing militarily; the temporary military elimination of Iraq will lead to a different equilibrium of relations in the Middle East but it is not likely to prove a stable equilibrium both while so many issues remain unresolved but while also the main military victor in this war contributes through uncritical support for Israel and a most likely vain effort to maintain the present regimes in the emirates to creating no small part of the region's political and military disequilibrium. Moreover, the alliance of states in the war followed closely, though obviously not exclusively, a fault line dividing the rich from the poor. Moreover, the military alliances in the eyes of Arab and Muslim populations followed a line dividing Arabs and Muslims from Christians and Westerners, and this further divide adds an embittering dimension to the previous cleavage. Finally, taking up arms too quickly is a poor way to establish a 'new world order' when one of the most critical issues of our time is to avoid war in a technological era in which traditional military defence offers less security than in previous eras of history and in which weapons of destruction have considerably outpaced means of defence.

There is a superficial sense in which the present American intervention resembles the gunboat diplomacy of the colonial period of the industrial revolution. The reality is however different and more serious.* The intervention may owe something to the mores of an earlier period but it is taking place in a world that has grown small, interdependent, and dangerous with new technological production, trade, and communication and that has begun to realise—without doing much that is constructive about it as yet—that world resources in their present forms of consumption are limited and that present patterns of consumption remain possible only because some three quarters of the world consume much less than its developed one quarter. It is significant that the present war is about access to a crucial resource, energy. Also, Third World countries have mostly looked on with resentment as a great and technologically developed country, the United States, has pounded the infra-structure of a poor country with a cruel and foolish leader into the dust. That example may well not be forgotten when new and more militarily powerful and revisionist contenders come on the scene—India and China, not least—and they will be better prepared to assert their claim to a share of global resources. They will have noted too the ready ruthlessness with which the leading Western country went to war to protect its interests.

In the last resort I could not bring myself to support this war or to judge it a just war† in spite of my rejection of the Iraqi annexation of Kuwait and desire to see it reversed. First, it began too soon and lost the opportunity of making sanctions work and enabling Arab and other brokerage to prove effective. Second, I cannot condone in terms of a principle of discrimination the tremendous destruction of the Iraqi economy—though I acknowl-

---

* There is a profound historical resemblance between the present American decision to undertake the Gulf war and the British and French decision to embark on the Suez expedition in that both actions stemmed from a failure to understand that crucial world changes had taken place and both decisions shared an anachronistic character.

† On the Iraqi side it is even more unjust: its regime had no just reason for annexing Kuwait; it did not sensibly negotiate before the war began; it made calculations of stupidity and folly in judging what would happen to its country and army; and it deliberately fired missiles against Israeli civilians as well as indiscriminately into Saudi Arabian cities.

edge a genuine attempt to avoid civilian deaths—that will harm Iraqi living standards and reduce life expectations for at least a generation among a poor people. Third, though various longer term objectives have been formulated—and they have mostly been formulated in a vague and generalised way—I believe that this war was started with myopic vision and with little understanding of its longer term effects as well as little grasp of the implications of contemporary global technology and political organization. In this connexion also great harm has been done to the legitimacy of the United Nations which has allowed its authority to be taken over by a partisan group of nations. The most that I can hope is that in those Western countries that have led this war, its mistaken and cruel nature will with time be recognized and appropriate conclusions drawn for participating in the construction of a more intelligent and just world order than the present breakdown of international order would appear to herald.

What Future for European Security?

*Eric Remacle**

The euphoria bred by German unification, and the seal of approval bestowed on the new European order by the Paris summit of the Conference on Security and Cooperation in Europe (CSCE) in November 1990, gave rise to the conviction that war would never again break out in Europe. Internal struggle within the Soviet Union and Yugoslavia has done little to shake this conviction, other than call for more measured enthusiasm. Yet no sooner have the wounds inflicted by the Cold War years begun to heal than an even more gaping sore has opened—this time in the Middle East and North Africa. These are territories branded by a succession of ill-fated and contradictory developments: the collapse of the Ottaman Empire, the claim to historic interests by the French and the British, the open sore of the Arab–Israeli conflict and the offensive inequality of the oil-rich Arab nations, on the one hand, and the mass of the Arab population on the other. What separates the two shores of the Mediterranean has been slowly but surely growing in political, economic and cultural complexity over the years. The Gulf war may yet turn out to be the catalyst for the long-awaited—and long overdue—collision between the Christian and Muslim worlds.

* Research fellow for the *Groupe de recherche et d'information sur la paix*—GRIP (Group for Research and Information for Peace) in Brussels.

Yalta redefined?

The sheer brutality of the Gulf tragedy requires us to take it seriously: failure to do so could prove fatal. Europe seems prepared to acknowledge the enormity of the crisis; nevertheless, its attitude during the Gulf war embittered many of those who had placed their trust in Europe's claim to a full and meaningful role in the regulation of the conflict. The contrast with the aftermath of the fall of the Berlin wall is only too stark: whereas the events of winter 1989 led to a prompt, efficient, and unanimous response on the part of the European Community, which accurately perceived itself as a future reference point for the countries of Eastern Europe, the Gulf war has seen the emergence of a timid and divided Community, its attention riveted—albeit anxiously—upon the United States. Europe in this instance has been visibly torn between a desire for further integration—common action in foreign and defence policy— and the maintenance of national sovereignty in these areas. Nowhere is the desire for national independence felt as strongly as in France and Great Britain, formerly colonial and now nuclear powers and therefore entitled, along with the United States, to both a permanent seat (and thus the right of veto) on the Security Council of the United Nations, and to a place in the club formed by the seven most industrialized nations of the world—G7. Perhaps it is simply that national sovereignty is now to be enshrined in a new Yalta built on the twin foundations of G7 and the UN Security Council; the former charged with policing the world economy, and the latter the world's security arrangements. This is a scenario more akin to the way in which the UN Charter was interpreted in 1945 than to our understanding of the same Charter in 1991.

Effectively excluded from any notion of leadership of such a new world order, Moscow is relegated to making diplomatic gestures whilst Bonn, Tokyo, and the European Community have been forced to swallow *de facto* affirmation of their status as political dwarf, legally constrained in the exercise of military force. Such is the context in which we must consider the Italian initiative of September 1990: that the European Community and Japan should henceforth be represented on the Security Council via the French and British seats.* Along with Rome's other proposal—the creation of a Conference on Security and Cooperation in the Mediterranean regions and the Middle East†—it promises an apparently novel approach to the institutional arrangements for the new international order; it is also in keeping with the momentum created by Europe's recent upheavals, in that it allows a radically alternative formulation of the concept of European and world security—one which is founded on the regulation of conflict by economic and political means rather than by the intervention of force. This is an interpretation of the world order which inextricably links together security, international cooperation, and human rights; as such it is appropriate to a world characterized by the increasing interdependence of national destinies, in particular due to the emerging non-military threats to our planet's survival: the destruction of the environment, the growing North–South divide, AIDS, the growth of organized crime, particularly in drugs, and so on. Because security, cooperation, and human rights are precisely the areas covered by the Helsinki Final Act's three 'baskets',‡ we lend credibility to the Helsinki agreements by understanding the world in this way, and by, for example, seeking to estabish 'common security', as did the Palme Committee in 1982§ or, in

* See *Le Monde*, Paris, 19 September, 1990, p.6 and 25 September, 1990, p.2. In a similar vein are the current Bonn proposals for a reform of the UN Security Council: one suggestion is that European Community member states rotate regularly in representing the Community on the Security Council; this was a proposal made by Willy Brandt (*Le Monde*, Paris, 19 February, 1991, p.5).

† We will come back to the proposal for a Conference on Security and Cooperation in the Mediterranean and the Middle East later in this article.

‡ Basket 1: European security; Basket 2; cooperation in the fields of the economy, science and technology and the environment; Basket 3: cooperation in human rights endeavours.

§ *Common Security. A Programme for Disarmament*, Pan Books, London, 1983.

the worlds of Karl Deutsch, a 'security community' on a world scale.*

It should come of little surprise that Europe is in the front line of this latest of battles. It is, after all, in Europe that the two most radically opposed visions of international relations are to be found: colonialism, Auschwitz, and Hiroshima on the one hand; the struggle for the emancipation of humankind, for human rights and freedom on the other. Only a year ago, Europe believed that it had finally come full circle—that it had come face to face with its destiny. It must now open a new chapter in its history which will allow it to readjust its relations with those of its neighbours who lie beyond the Mediterranean. Its success— or failure—in doing so will determine the future of the North– South relationship. This is why the Gulf war has heightened our hopes and fears concerning Europe's role in our new world order and justifies a detailed analysis of Europe's approach to the war, its internal divisions and their consequences.

Europe and the Gulf: disarray or a US-dictated division of labour?

A first remark to be made is that the Europe which has taken a stand and made its voice known, in this crisis as in many others, is not the larger Europe—extending from the Atlantic to the Urals—which was ushered in at the Paris Summit of November 1990: the Foreign Ministers of the CSCE nations only

---

* Karl Deutsch coined the term 'security community' in 1953, defining it as follows: 'a group which has become integrated, where integration is defined as the attainment of a sense of community, accompanied by formal or informal institutions or practices, sufficiently strong and widespread to assure peaceful change among members of a group with "reasonable" certainty over a "long" period of time.' It is a notion that was invoked on several occasions in 1990 to denote the ideal goal for Europe. See Bertrand, Maurice, 'Quelles nouvelles fonctions pour l'OTAN et le Pacte de Varsovie? Les dangers d'une "Communauté de sécurité"', *Le Monde diplomatique*, Paris, February, 1990, pp. 6–7; Blackaby, Frank, *A New Security Structure for Europe*, BASIC, London and Washington DC, June, 1990; Eyskens, Mark, *Une Charte européenne de sécurité*, Belgian Ministry for Foreign Affairs, Brussels, June, 1990.

ever met once in the context of the Gulf crisis, and this in itself was a breakthrough. They met in extraordinary session parallel to the UN General Assembly structure on 1 and 2 October, 1990, and issued a joint declaration on the Gulf crisis, condemning the Iraqi invasion and occupation of Kuwait and supporting all initiatives aimed at resolving the conflict and bringing about a fair, global, and durable peace settlement which fully respected the UN Security Council resolutions.* At the Paris Summit itself, although it took place only one week before the adoption of Resolution 678, the question of the Gulf crisis did not find its way onto the agenda. Of the seventeen non-NATO members of the CSCE and the European Community, only Poland and Czechoslovakia made even a symbolic contribution to the multinational force stationed in Saudi Arabia; all the others simply held the embargo laid down by Security Council Resolution 661; nevertheless, these countries did include Switzerland, which was taking such action for the first time. Finland too saw fit to modify its interpretation of the notion of neutrality by taking over the presidency of the Sanctions Committee set up by Resolution 661.

We do not intend to address the question of the Soviet Union in any detail here. What we can say is that the only European countries to take political and/or military action were those that were already members of NATO and of the European Community. We can identify five distinct channels via which these countries' action in the Gulf was implemented: national policy decisions (of the fifteen nations concerned); bilateral agreements between these countries and the USA (governing, in particular, military bases on their territories); NATO; the European Community; the Western European Union (WEU). What may appear to be a rather haphazard and wasteful organization of the Europeans' efforts was in fact a well-coordinated arrangement, designed to fit in closely with US objectives and to stave off any possible claim by the Europeans to a common and independent European policy. We should add that it would, in any case, have proved extremely

*Cited in *Focus on Vienna*, p.3. No. 20, The Austrian Committee for European Security and Cooperation, Vienna, October, 1990.

difficult to have achieved a coordinated European response, given the diversity of organizations involved and the differences in their membership: fourteen of the countries belong to the Atlantic Alliance;* twelve are part of its integrated command structure;† twelve (but not the same twelve) are members of the Community,‡ and nine make up the WEU.§ This is a situation which favours independent national action and which, in fact, very probably made it easier for certain of the participants to limit the extent of their involvement in a conflict which they were not convinced was entirely justified. For example, four countries—Germany, Belgium, Spain, and Portugal—openly restricted their Gulf participation to the provision of logistical and purely defensive support, in response to pressure from public opinion hostile to any military role. In choosing to restrict their intervention in this way, these particular countries effectively placed the satisfaction of the national interest above any desire to have a say in the military decisions taken during the course of the conflict. This was because Security Council Resolution 678 did not oblige the anti-Iraq coalition to rally under the UN banner;¶ nor did the Soviet plan for coordination under the Military Chief-of-Staff Committee of the UN get off the ground. As a result, only those nations directly participating in the war effort in Saudi Arabia and in Kuwait could take part in the political and military decision making process. This left the other European countries with the freedom only to bargain over the upper limit of their involvement in a military operation orchestrated by the USA.

That the scope for action in the field of defence and security is different for each of the European Community, NATO, and

* Belgium, Denmark, France, Germany, Greece, Iceland, Italy, Luxemburg, the Netherlands, Norway, Portugal, Spain, Turkey, United Kingdom.

† France and Spain are not part of NATO's integrated command structure.

‡ The fourteen NATO members minus Iceland, Norway and Turkey and plus Ireland, which is neutral.

§ Belgium, France, Germany, Italy, Luxemburg, the Netherlands, Portugal, Spain, and the United Kingdom.

¶ The resolution authorizes member states to use all necessary means in ensuring the respect and application of Resolution 660.

WEU, was a contributory factor to the situation described above. European Political Cooperation (EPC) within the Community is only, at present, enabled to handle the political and economic aspects of security policy;* furthermore, EPC decisions must be reached by consensus (i.e. all twelve Community member states must agree). EPC declarations were issued condemning Iraq,† supporting the UN resolutions and embargo, approving humanitarian aid to the innocent victims of sanctions, protesting against the Iraqi use of non-Iraqi citizens as a 'human shield', and ordering the closure of the Community nations' embassies in Kuwait City. A limited number of small scale diplomatic initiatives were also taken under EPC; we shall come to these below.

WEU‡ action consisted in coordinating the sailing of naval vessels to the area of conflict in order to enforce the UN embargo.§ Based on its experience of similar operations during the Iraq–Iran war in 1987–88, the WEU attempted to improve the quality of its coordinating role in this instance. The most notable manifestation of this was that on 17 August 1990, the WEU arranged its first ever meeting of the Chiefs of Staff of its

---

* See the Single European Act, Title III, Art. 30, 6a.

† EPC consultations under the Italian presidency were held on 2, 4, 10 and 21 August, 7 and 17 September and on 5 November and 18 December. Two further meetings took place at the beginning of the Luxemburg presidency, on 4 and 17 January. In addition, the European Council met twice, once on 28 October and the second time on 14–15 December; both Councils were held in Rome.

‡ The Council of Ministers of the WEU met in Paris on 21 August, 18 September, 10 December and 17 January; France held the presidency on all occasions.

§ The WEU deployed fifty ships and approximately twelve thousand men in the Gulf and in the Gulf of Oman. The force included French troops stationed in Djibouti; Denmark and Greece, both EC but not WEU members, sent one vessel each to the region. Two Italian corvettes were held on standby in the Mediterranean, as were one aircraft carrier, two frigates and one French tanker off the coast of Toulon. Germany was prevented by its Constitution from sending troups beyond NATO limits but sent six vessels to the Mediterranean to replace those belonging to its allies which had departed for the Gulf. Luxemburg does not possess a national fleet but provided financial support to the WEU's war effort (4 million dollars—January, 1991).

member nations under the presidency of the French. Even so, it was a superficial role, in that the most important decisions had already been taken by individual member states; moreover, disagreements concerning the relative status of the UN resolutions on the one hand, and WEU action on the other, and the status of the WEU in relation to US operations, were visible despite the veneer of coordination and cooperation.* From 18 September onwards, at the request of the French and the British, WEU military coordination was extended to cover ground and air forces, and logistical activity; the WEU simultaneously requested that sanctions be extended to airborne traffic.† Such initiatives did demonstrate that the European nations could exert joint pressure on the UN Security Council, provided that the political will to do so existed in the first place.

NATO is not authorized to take military action outside the geographical area defined by Article 6 of the Washington Treaty.‡ So its role in the Gulf conflict only extended to three clearly-defined domains.§ Firstly, it was able to confirm its solidarity

---

* The WEU communiqué of 21 August, 1990 makes these disagreements plain. It does not state unequivocally that the WEU would respect UN decisions (as the Germans and Belgium would have wanted). Instead, it makes vague references to European interests in the Gulf (thereby satisfying the British condition: that intervention outside UN-sanctioned action remain possible). Moreover, paragraph 9 of the communiqué emphasises the fact that WEU-coordinated action should also facilitate cooperation with other nations deploying forces in the region, and in particular with the USA.

† This request was effectively granted one week later by the passing of UN resolution 670.

‡ '[...] an armed attack on one or more of the Parties is deemed to include an armed attack
● on the territories of any of the Parties in Europe or North America, on the territory of Turkey or on the Islands under the jurisdiction of any of the Parties in the North Atlantic area north of the Tropic of Cancer;
● on the forces, vessels or aircraft of any of the Parties, when in or over these territories or any other area in Europe in which occupation forces of any of the Parties were stationed on the date when the Treaty entered into force or the Mediterranean Sea or the North Atlantic area north of the Tropic of Cancer'.

§ The North Atlantic Council met in ministerial session on 10 August, 10 September, and 17 and 18 December. The Defence Planning Committee (of which France is not a member) met on 6 and 7 December at ministerial level.

with Turkey, Iraq's neighbour and anxious to defend itself against a possible Iraqi attack. Secondly, NATO provided logistical support to the American forces in the Gulf. Thirdly, it coordinated the sailing of the eight NATO Mediterranean command ships, of mine-sweepers from the Channel fleet, and of the NATO Channel Command to the eastern Mediterranean; this was to compensate for the previous departure of several vessels belonging to the Gulf states from the Mediterranean to the Gulf, the Red Sea, and the Gulf of Oman, and in order to send out a political signal: that NATO was wholehearted about protecting its Parties' territories.

The logic of war: a series of *faits accomplis*

Even though it may seem from what has been said that the Europeans responded unanimously to the Gulf crisis, this was only the case for decisions taken on logistical and support matters. When it came to sending troops, there was strictly no consultation, whether initiated from the United States, France, or the UK. What is more, each critical decision was taken unilaterally *before* joint political meetings on the subject had even got underway. For example, President Bush's announcement on 8 August that American GIs were to be sent to Saudi Arabia was followed by decisions taken in London and Paris the following day to send reinforcements to their naval and air forces in the region. All that the European Community and NATO ministerial sessions, held on 10 August, could then do was to formally record that the decisions had been taken. Similarly, François Mitterrand effectively presented his European partners with a *fait accompli* when, on 21 August, he made public his intention to send ground forces to Saudi Arabia and to the United Emirates, in response to what he called the Iraqi 'logic of war'. Exactly the same thing was to happen when the USA went ahead with the reinforcement of its military presence in the

Gulf;* this included the announcement made in Washington between the 8 and 9 November to sanction the sending of an additional 200,000 men and women to the crisis zone and to go ahead with its 'Imminent Thunder' strategy. This particular move was a clear signal—twenty days before the Security Council passed Resolution 678—of the United States' intention to resort to force to liberate Kuwait.

Nevertheless, constant use was made all along of the various multinational organizations (the EC, the WEU, and NATO) in order to solicit allied support for the war effort of the three permanent members of the Security Council. On the first occasions that the Americans approached NATO for this purpose (3 September), certain of its European members (notably Germany, Spain, and Holland), gave only a guarded response.† They were to react more favourably only when, one week later, James Baker presented European nations with his list of concrete options for which shared responsibility was required. It was a move which, due to the diversity of the tasks it outlined, enabled each of the Allies to make an independent *national* choice as to the extent of their commitment to the war effort. Thus Belgium and Norway were able to assist with the evacuation of refugees; Germany made much of the economic aid it provided to the countries of central and eastern Europe adversely affected by the embargo on Iraq. Also on the shopping list was the escalation

---

* In total, the number of European ground and air forces that had been sent to the countries belonging to the Gulf Cooperation Council (Bahrain, Qatar, Kuwait, Saudi Arabia, Oman and the United Arab Emirates) by 17 January was as follows: 43,000 men (32,000 British; 11,000 French and 270 Italian); 203 heavy tanks, 159 light tanks, 246 troop transport vehicles, 160 helicopters and 139 fighter planes. By way of comparison, the US had sent 365,000 men and women, 2,000 tanks, 1,280 troop transport vehicles, 1,500 helicopters and 1,300 fighter planes. (*source:* GRIP DATA).

† The Netherlands were particularly concerned to establish whether the American request was in keeping with Article 51 of the United Nations Charter (*Nouvelles atlantiques*, no. 2251, Agence Europe, Brussels, 8 September, 1990).

of manoeuvres by the Alliance's multinational forces, the provision of help to Egypt and Turkey, the supply of air and naval
equipment for the transportation of American troops, and, finally,
the sending of additional ground forces.* It was a method of
gaining support that was again employed within NATO following
the 8 November decision to send out more US troops; the French
and the British subsequently used very similar means on several
occasions within the WEU framework.

It is worth pointing here to a further example of the ambiguity
inherent in the whole allied decision-making process. It concerns
the question of allied support for Turkey. The subject had come
up on the agenda of several of the Allies' political sessions ever
since 10 August. Ankara, however, waited until the beginning
of December before calling on the Allies for help;† it was largely,
we suspect, the passing of Resolution 678 which managed to
convince President Ozal that armed conflict in the Gulf had now
become inevitable. For the first time ever in the history of
NATO, Turkey formally asked its Allies for assistance, while
simultaneously stressing its own non-offensive intentions and its
view that the crisis should ultimately be handled by means of a
regional Middle East security and cooperation dialogue.‡ On 21
December, the Defence Planning Committee set in motion the
decision-making machinery which would lead to the sending of
the Allied Mobile Force air forces: eighteen German Alphajets,
eighteen Belgian Mirage-Vs and six Italian Starfighter F-104s.
German and Belgian hesitation at a move of this kind which
implied possible direct military action against Iraq culminated in
missions being despatched from Bonn to Brussels to assess the

* It was at this juncture that Italy went ahead with the decision to send
Tornado fighter-bombers to Saudi Arabia.
† Even in November the Turkish government had turned down the
proposal from the Hague to deploy a squadron of F-16 fighter-bombers in
Turkey to help hold the air embargo.
‡ Turgut Ozal, 'Turkey: An Unwanted War Became Unavoidable', *Inter-
national Herald Tribune*, Paris, 3 January, 1991.

situation in Turkey before finally accepting Ankara's request on 2 January—but on the condition that their forces were to be used only for defensive operations.* Similar reservations found expression in the rules of engagement drawn up and adopted by the Defence Planning Committee on 8 January; the rules emphasize, indeed insist, on the strictly defensive mandate of the multinational force and on the necessity for the force both to refrain from provocative action and to avoid incidents wherever possible; the Allies' pilots were, nevertheless, authorized to launch counter-attacks against enemy aggression—in the name of self-defence.†

Shortly after war broke out on 17 January, President Ozal won the Turkish parliament's approval—by 250 votes to 148— to authorize American air forces to use Turkish territory for the launching of their bombing missions on Iraq. It was a unilateral decision taken only under the auspices of the USA–Turkey defence agreement; in other words, it was not put to the Allies for approval. The Turkish opposition insisted that this in fact amounted to the opening of a second front,‡ while in Germany, military experts with close links to the SPD denounced the move as an act of provocation.§ Reactions such as these highlight the fact that the decision was yet another *fait accompli* which provided for the imposition of a unilateral position on all other parties by virtue of the fact that the letter of the treaties concerned had, in fact, been respected. Article 5 of the Washington Treaty does not commit its signatories to the doctrine of mutual defence of

---

* 'Brussels et Bonn s'appuient sur une structure défensive de l'OTAN', *Le Soir*, Brussels, 3 January, 1991.

† *Nouvelles atlantiques*, no. 2287, p.1. Agence Europe, Brussels, 11 January, 1991.

‡ Nicole Pope, 'L'aviation américaine pourra utiliser le territoire turc', *Le Monde*, 19 January, 1991.

§ *Nouvelles atlantiques*, no. 2291, p.2. Agence Europe, Brussels, 23 January, 1991.

NATO members;* nevertheless, considerable pressure was exerted on Bonn and Brussels to accept the principle of mutual assistance, with the result that any action to the contrary would soon have run the risk of placing considerable strain on the Atlantic Alliance precisely at a point when, for the first time in its forty-two year existence, its solidarity was being put to the test.

The same could be said of other bilateral decisions taken during the conflict such as the agreement to allow American B-52 bombers to use air bases in Spain, Greece, the UK, and the Azores, and to use French air space as required. Decisions such as these only serve to highlight the perversity of a security system in which the United Nations effectively grants *carte blanche* to Washington, London, and Paris in the implementation of Article 51 of the UN Charter. Moreover, it clearly points to the ambiguities inherent in a military arrangement which allows three permanent members of the Security Council to make unilateral decisions on military action, for which they then proceed to canvass support from their allies via a myriad of bilateral accords and multinational organizations overlapping in their membership and scope for action (NATO, the WEU and the EC).

The whole issue begs the question of whether the time has not in fact come to review both the way in which the Security Council works, and the decision-making process within the Atlantic Alliance. It seems to us that at the heart of any reform lies the future role of the Community: only a more confident

---

* The Parties agree that an armed attack against one or more of them in Europe or North America shall be considered an attack against them all and consequently they agree that, if such an attack occurs, each of them, in exercise of the right of individual or collective self-defence recognized by Article 51 of the Charter of the United Nations, will assist the Party or Parties so attacked by taking forthwith, individually and in concert with the other Parties, such action as it deems necessary, including the use of armed force to restore and maintain the security of the North Atlantic area. Any such armed attack and all measures taken as a result thereof shall immediately be reported to the Security Council. Such measures shall be terminated when the Security Council has taken the measures necessary to restore and maintain international peace and security.

and unified European Community, speaking with one voice in external affairs could ensure that future independentist and fanciful French and British ideas are channelled into positive policy decisions and, into the bargain, counterbalance the lone leadership of whichever superpower emerges victorious from the post-cold war age.

The European Community: in search of a common foreign policy

Even before the invasion of Kuwait, the tumultuous events of central and eastern Europe had raised many questions amongst the twelve Community member states: the situation seemed to demand further integration, possibly towards the federal model, and notably in the fields of economic and monetary union on the one hand, and political union—meaning a common foreign, defence, and security policy—on the other.* Far from slowing down the process of European unification, the Gulf crisis has acted as catalyst and accelerator. As early as 10 August, Italy—which at the time held the presidency of the Community—made Community history by calling for an extraordinary session of Community Foreign ministers meeting under the European Political Cooperation procedure, to take place *before* the meeting of NATO foreign ministers. Gianni de Michelis, Italy's Foreign minister, was quick to point out the political significance of the chronological order of these two meetings; it was, moreover, a move which perfectly symbolized the desire of the Italians to see the Community constitute the European security pillar of the Atlantic Alliance. In a memorandum released by the Italian presidency in November, this vision was reaffirmed;† the memorandum effectively sought to enlarge the scope for joint Community action, in particular in areas which had hitherto been

* Readers are referred to the author's own article: 'Les Douze en quête d'une politique étrangère et de sécurité commune', to be published in *Etudes internationales*, Quebec, Canada.

† In a document published by *The Guardian*, 22 November, 1990.

reserved for NATO—disarmament, for example—or for the
WEU, such as military initiatives carried out under the auspices
of the UN. In addition, the memorandum outlined a plan to
merge the WEU and the Community in 1998 after a transitional
period during which cooperation between the two organizations
would progressively increase; it also suggested that the proposed
new Treaty on Political Union should contain a clause enshrining
the principle of automatic mutual military assistance, similar to
that contained in the founding treaty of the WEU. This is an idea
that the Commission of the European Communities took up in
their opinion published on 21 October, 1990, in which the
Commission put forward the idea of abolishing Article 223 of
the Rome Treaty, thus clearing the way for joint action in arms
production and control.* At the same time, the Italians and the
Spanish—supported by Jacques Delors and the majority of their
Community partners (with the notable exception of the UK)—
floated the notion of a Conference on Mediterranean and Middle
East Security and Cooperation, the idea being that this would
provide a forum for the diplomatic regulation of future conflicts
in the region; it would, moreover, be complementary to both
the Europe–Arab dialogue (relaunched in 1989) and to the
international conference on the Arab–Israeli conflict called for
by the Community as early as 1980 in its Venice summit
declaration. Part of the preparation for the European Council
Rome summit of 14 and 15 December (itself the prelude to the
launching of the intergovernmental conference on political union)
was therefore given over to paving the way for a common
foreign policy, the significant development being that this policy
would henceforth be developed within the traditional (i.e.
Treaty-based) Community framework rather than the alternative
European Political Cooperation procedure (based on consensus
decisions between the governments of the twelve Community
states). This preparatory work covered all the main elements
of a future joint Community policy for the Middle East: a

* *Union politique*. Commission of the European Communities, Brussels, 21
October 1990.

reformulation of NATO rules in favour of the European powers; increased autonomy for Europe *vis-à-vis* Washington; a role for Europe in the peace-keeping UN force; a common defence policy; Community control of arms exports and of the non-proliferation of ballistic, chemical, and nuclear weapons; finally, the launching of an international peace conference on the Middle East, of the Conference for Mediterranean and Middle East Security and Cooperation, and of a Europe–Arab dialogue.*

Despite this impressive display of proposed unity, the Twelve failed to take common action at various points during the Gulf crisis. Britain and France's preference for autonomy is already known to us here; so is that fact that Italy and the Netherlands were prepared to provide military back-up to the British and French effort whilst Germany, Belgium, Spain, Portugal, Greece, and Denmark sought to contain their contribution to the actual war effort. Ireland too extended support only to the point of allowing its Shannon airport to be used for refuelling by American planes en route for the Gulf; Luxemburg limited its participation to channelling financial aid to the war effort via the WEU. It is worth probing deeper into the German response: Bonn was unable, constitutionally, to despatch troops anywhere outside NATO limits; it was also under considerable strain as a result of unification. For these reasons, Germany did not play a major role in the crisis. It was both for historical reasons, and out of regard for its neighbouring territories, that Kohl sought to play down any military role for Germany, and to promote instead an image of Germany as the pacifist paymaster of the new world order, which would stand aside while others kept world peace through the enforcement of international law. Public opinion against German military involvement may yet prove to be so strong as to persuade both Chancellor Kohl and Hans-Dietrich Genscher to drop the plan which they subsequently

---

* The same ideas (albeit couched in slightly different terms) reappear in the letter sent by François Mitterrand and Helmut Kohl to the Italian presidency on 6 December (and published in *Le Monde*, Paris, 10 December, 1990), in Douglas Hurd's speech to the Berlin Press Club on 10 December and in the Luxemburg presidency proposals made on 16 January, 1991.

unveiled to the WEU Council on 21 August, namely, to write into the planned Constitution for the new unified Germany a clause permitting a German military contribution to UN forces. But we should also bear in mind that Germany's recent past ensures great reluctance in Bonn to make choices in foreign policy that fundamentally contradict American policy.* This is why Germany, in the Gulf crisis, sought to avoid US retribution by agreeing to send battleships to the eastern Mediterranean under the auspices of the WEU and by taking part in NATO-operated multilateral operations (NATO Mediterranean and Channel commands in the Mediterranean; Allied Mobile Forces in Turkey). The bulk of Bonn's contribution was nevertheless financial: it provided DM 10 billion worth of funds and equipment to the US, 1 billion to the UK, one and a quarter million to Israel (including the shipment of specialized armoured tanks for the detection of NBC weapons, and of Patriot missiles). DM 2.3 million were also spread between Jordan, Egypt, and Turkey; in addition, Bonn underwrote 20% of the cost of the humanitarian and economic aid programme made available by the Community to countries of the Gulf region suffering hardship as a result of the crisis.† A final plank to Bonn's contribution—an undertaking to tighten its controls on the export of arms, and of military and chemical equipment or know-how to the Middle East‡—arose from the blow delivered to the German administration by revelations of the extent of involvement of German companies in providing Saddam Hussein and his regime with military equipment and technology, and with products used in the manufacture of chemical weapons.

The Community's internal disagreements were displayed most acutely over the question of the foreign hostages held in Baghdad. On 28 October, the European Council issued a declaration that

* Paul-Marie de la Gorce, 'L'éclatante démission de la diplomatie européenne', *Le Monde diplomatique*, p.6. Paris, February, 1991.

† See 'Ceux qui ne donnent pas de troupes mais de l'argent', *Le Soir*, Brussels, 4 February, 1991.

‡ This included shipments to members of the allied coalition: in October 1990, for example, Germany refused to deliver weapons to Saudi Arabia.

the Twelve Community member states would refuse to engage in separate negotiations with Baghdad for the release of the hostages. However, on 4 November, the German government eventually reneged on an earlier decision it had made—as well as that of 28 October—and gave Willy Brandt the go-ahead to make his 'humanitarian' mission to Baghdad. This was in the wake of the Iraqi decision, made on 29 October, to release the remaining French hostages in response, it can be assumed, not just to the diplomatic manoeuverings of President François Mitterrand but also to the secret mission undertaken by Claude Cheysson. So when Hans-Dietrich Genscher put forward his proposal, on 5 November, that the Community should attempt to persuade Saddam Hussein to allow a UN mission to go to Iraq to secure the release of all remaining hostages (the Iraqi government failed to grant the request, when it was made), the Community's positive response really represented no more than a facade of unity.

Even the Community's attempts to formulate a diplomatic solution to the crisis did not run entirely smoothly. There *was* agreement that Iraq should be required to leave Kuwait in exchange for the commitment not to take military action against Saddam Hussein;* nevertheless, at Luxemburg on 4 January, the most the Community Foreign ministers could do was to reiterate their joint pledge to contribute in full to the resolution of outstanding problems in the region and to establish, in the Middle East, a climate of security, stability, and development once the current crisis had been solved by peaceful means and with full regard for Security Council resolutions. This was a particularly vague statement based on a visibly shaky compromise, in that it did not contain the promise to hold either one, or several, international peace conference(s), as had been suggested by the French but rejected by the British and the Dutch. In fact, the French diplomatic initiative, encapsulated in its peace plan put to the UN General Assembly on 24 September,

---

*France, Spain, Belgium, and Germany, as well as the Soviet Union, insisted on this particular commitment.

was doomed to fail, even though it seemed highly promising. This was because the plan was to be enacted within the framework of those organizations whose member states dispose—either constitutionally or *de facto*—of the right of veto: the Security Council of the UN and the Community's EPC structure. It was for exactly the same reason that the last-minute French proposal for a diplomatic solution (put to the Security Council on 15 January) could not be sure of British and American support—which it did not get. On the eve of the deadline for the Iraqis to retreat from Kuwait, the French and the British in fact proposed two different resolutions, only to subsequently have to withdraw them for fear of the consequences of displaying too openly the cracks in the international community at such a crucial point in time. The disarray of the Community was far more visible, as the UK went to no pains to hide its willingness to act as errand boy for the White House.

We should not be surprised that the British employed tactics such as these: there was an early precedent. When on 18 December it appeared that the USA and Iraq would never agree on a date for a Baker–Aziz summit, the North Atlantic Council somewhat hypocritically gave the go-ahead for an independent Community initiative. Gianni de Michelis subsequently proposed that a meeting between Tarik Aziz and Community representatives should be arranged. Great Britain promptly rejected the idea in principle.* All de Michelis could do to retrieve the situation was to note that for the first time ever, the Atlantic alliance had at least recognized the principle of specific Community initiatives; he also proposed that the Twelve reconvene in early January to discuss the possibility of a Community move if, by then, it had become clear that there would be no direct US–Iraqi meetings and/or discussions. 18 December, 1990 in fact marks the day when the Community could have intervened to change the course of the Gulf conflict—but failed to do so. When the Community finally did invite the Iraqi foreign minister to a meeting with his Community counterparts in Geneva on 4 January, the fact that

* Britain was supported by Luxemburg and the Netherlands in their refusal.

the invitation came hot on the heels of the Baker–Tariz meeting, and that it made transparent the extent to which the Community felt compelled—largely by the UK—to follow the US line, did not go unnoticed by Tarik Aziz—who declined the invitation.

Our conclusion is twofold. Firstly, the Gulf crisis served to strengthen US leadership of the Western world and to demonstrate that, far from seeking to play the role of European 'federator', as suggested and feared by de Gaulle in earlier days, the US was only too happy to play on differences of opinion within the European Community in order to ensure that its own interests prevailed. Secondly, by virtue of both their permanent representation on the UN Security Council and the inevitable logic of war itself, France and Britain reinvoked—and reinforced—their claims to national sovereignty, effectively ignoring the current drift towards European integration as they did so *and* taking the opportunity to redress the balance within Europe, in favour of London and Paris, and against Bonn. The consequences of such behaviour are already making themselves felt.

Justice and the Arab World

Buhram Ghalioun*

The war in the Gulf has shown the importance of the spiritual, ideological, and political differences which set the Western states in opposition to the Arab world. After more than a month of fighting, in which the death toll is amongst the highest in the history of the human race, the positions of the two sides remain unchanged. It is not certain that the future outcome of this war will be able to influence in any way the claims being made by each side in terms of the causes of the war, of the issues at stake, and of the real objectives and the consequences of this major conflict of the latter part of the twentieth century. The coalition powers, and in particular those of the West, continue to proclaim the concept of a just war, on the basis of the enforcement of international law: to this claim, the Arabs will oppose the concept of a pre-determined intention to destroy the Iraqi military potential in order to maintain control over the oil-wealth, to reduce its cost, and to ensure Israeli military domination in the region. For the Arabs, this automatically points to a maintenance of the status quo, which means a return to an intolerable situation of strategic stalemate with regard to the search for a solution to the Palestinian tragedy, the continuing economic collapse, the absence of cooperation between rich and poor Arab countries, and the reinforcement of a system of political oppression based

* Syrian writer and politician, author of several works on the politics of the Arab world, and author of *Le Malaise des Arabes, L'Etat contre la nation.* Paris, La Découverte, forthcoming.

on an agreement on security, with unpopular regimes supported by foreign aid.

Are the Arabs, who never cease to cry out for justice, so insensitive to the concept of law? Is the West, which never ceases to proclaim its championship of the principles of peace, security, prosperity, and democracy, so insensitive to the sufferings of the Arab world? Through the opposition of the West to the Arab world, which the current war has revealed and amplified, this misunderstanding on such a large-scale poses the fundamental question of the rules which regulate international relations, at a time when not only are colonial-type relationships no longer valid, but the concept of absolute sovereignty also tends to be submerged in the melting-pot of a global policy for the future of the world.

The welcome insistence by the West on the power of the law doubtless originates from the growing need and sense of urgency, experienced by all nations, for the establishment of a world order which will guarantee peace and stability. On the other hand, the reticence of the Arabs, Muslims, and perhaps of the whole of the Third World, in the face of this world order, is locked into a feeling of insecurity, which is reinforced by decades, if not centuries, of oppression and injustice, often perpetrated in the name of the law. That is why, behind this historic duel, the fundamental issue of the present confrontation is that of the definition of the very substance of international law, which constitutes, or should constitute, the rules of engagement for any order which does not simply seek to impose the will of the strongest. Does the organization of the United Nations, as constituted after the Allied victory, represent the seat of power of an international legislative body? Are the means at its disposal sufficient to guarantee the impartial enforcement of its decisions? Even more importantly, do all peoples and nations have a genuine opportunity to make their voices heard in the face of international power-games, political maneouvres and the might of dictatorships? In short, what kind of world order are we talking about? What is the underlying philosophy of this order, and on what moral and political principles can it be founded?

The concept of political interest

Unless one views politics through rose-coloured glasses, the military intervention by the coalition forces, like that of Iraq in Kuwait, can only be motivated by vested interest. However, the need to identify national or individual interests does not figure in the ethical code of our modern, unethical world. On the contrary, it is the source of rationalization of conflicts, in so far as it bases policies on a more easily-identifiable and negotiable concept. It is, moreover, the basis for the great progress achieved by the human race in the field of national policies. This principle is not, therefore, open to discussion. Rather, it is the intention to conceal true interests behind general moralistic principles which should make us doubt the good intentions of others. What is equally open to discussion is the legitimacy of both the nature of this interest and of the means used to further it. This is the starting-point from which the behaviour of nations can be judged, from a moral and from a political viewpoint.

Iraq was not censured because of its claims concerning the realignment of frontiers and the writing off of its debt, which were morally and politically negotiable, but rather by the way in which it went about this; namely, the use of large-scale force and occupation. As for the United States and the other Western countries in the coalition, if the upholding of a certain, moderate oil-policy constitutes a legitimate interest in itself, many questions remain as to the definition of how it should be formulated, and what measures should be adopted to ensure its observance. For example, what would constitute a guarantee of the oil supply for industrialized countries and what price levels would best meet their legitimate interests? Would they agree to reach these through a negotiated settlement with oil-producing countries, or would they expect to use all available means, including war and the Security Council, to achieve their objectives?

The principle of negotiation

The only acceptable rule is one which involves the recognition in law of reciprocity of interests, and of an agreement by

consensus in order to implement these interests. It is only in this
way that any modification of interests can be achieved. As soon
as the vital interests of one partner to a contract are denied, there
is a risk of rebellion, and violent conflict becomes the only
possible outcome of the dispute. This is the situation which the
United States sought to create in the Gulf, in order to achieve
predetermined objectives.

The most prominent factor in all this, which has constituted
the prime issue at the root of the Gulf crisis, is the existence on
the one hand of a fierce determination by Iraq to impose the
principle of negotiation as a means of regulating the problems
of the Middle East, and on the other hand, the refusal of the
United States, unlike the other powers, to negotiate, and their
fierce determination to condemn all initiatives for dialogue or
negotiation, whether these come from the Europeans, the Arabs,
or the Iraqis themselves.* In their refusal, the US is not only
hitting at Iraq, but also, during this period of transition, at the
rest of the world as it attempts to solve the thorny problem of
the introduction of new ground rules for international politics,
which are intended to obtain for decades to come.

In fact, as the present situation shows, there is a temptation,
when self-esteem is based on contempt or under-estimation of
the value of others, to confuse personal interest with that of the
law, thus completely blocking any possibility of negotiation.
This has been the traditional American position with regard to
all attempts at world negotiation between North and South,
whether the issue was one relating to raw materials, to the new
world economic order, or to information and projects relating
to collective security.

The acceptance of dialogue with a Third World country would
straight away have implied the birth of a new world order based
on concerted effort, which is an as yet underdeveloped area, and

---

*It goes without saying that the two most important victims of this
attitude, in the field of international diplomacy, are the Arab League and the
United Nations Organization, which have both been used as instruments to
cover up and legitimize the American intervention. As a result, they are
completely discredited.

so would bring into question the present order, based on the marginalization and the exclusion of the Third World and thus, in other words, of three-quarters of the human race. Moreover, this explains the ease with which Washington finally managed to draw everyone in the Western world into the same boat, and why a relatively unimportant conflict over borders became the cause of major confrontation between two cultures and civilizations, and even between North and South.

In truth, when faced on the one hand with an unbelievable escalation of the political and economic problems of the Third World, and on the other hand, with the absence of any overall conception of the immediate future of the human race, as well as the lack of coherent policies for this, the bloc of First World countries does not wish to risk the opening up of a dialogue which could only lead to its having to agree to major concessions in order to quell a rebellion which might be fermenting on the periphery of its sphere of interest. As the custodian of inter-national law, the industrialized bloc thus seeks to protect in advance, if not to justify, any future interventions it might undertake. Furthermore, at the same time as the Americans are displaying their desire to impose themselves as a world-sheriff, they are manipulating the United Nations in the process, and transforming the whole of the Third World into a zone which is potentially beyond the protection of the law.

The blatant refusal to negotiate, as demonstrated by Washing-ton, and the blocking of any political solution, symbolize the criteria by which America intends to establish its rule of generalized world dominance, the new American order. In order to achieve this, there are two objectives to be pursued. Firstly, to assert American leadership in the face of rival economic powers, namely those of Japan and Europe. And secondly to fill, in the eyes of the rest of the world, the gap left by the withdrawal of the Soviet Union from the strategic contest for domination of the planet. Now that the United States occupy, unchallenged, first place in the superpower league, they could become unchallengeable.

From this aspect, and according to the logic of challenge and of recourse to extreme measures, the Gulf crisis constitutes a model for future insoluble clashes, which will bring into opposition the bloc of highly-industrialized countries and the small but growing powers of the Third World.

Vital interests of the Arabs

It will be hard to achieve any degree of understanding between the Arabs and the West if each side does not attempt to identify somewhat more precisely what it considers to be its strategic or vital interests. For the Arabs, these can be grouped into three categories: those interests linked to the economic and political integration of the Arab world, as a vector for peace and stability in the region; those interests relating to national and collective security, which include the Palestinian question and the Israeli–Arab conflict; and finally, economic and social development with its concomitant requirements of control of national resources, of the acquisition of modern technology and training. Unfortunately, on all these fronts the needs of the Arab societies for regional cooperation, for security and development, either go unrecognized or are deliberately ignored.

The search by the Arab world for its unity has been systematically denigrated and wrongly interpreted. The very idea of union, or of the Arab nation, is subject to suspicion. On countless occasions, politicians and media representatives, not to mention the intellectual élite, have been heard to accuse Arab nationalism of being illusory, irrational, dangerous, and even fascist in nature.* Most people have heard that ardent supporter of European unity, Jacques Delors, proclaim on television, at

---

*For example: Alain Touraine: 'The Language of Dictators', *Le Monde*, 10 February, 1991, in which he confuses Islam with Arabism: 'Today, calls to an Arab nation or to Islam only serve to illustrate this tendency to replacement by a nationalist or ideological dictatorship. Those who define the present conflict as a clash between Islam and Christianity, between the Arabs and the Western world, or even between East and West, whether deliberately or not, are using the language of new-style dictatorships, which is also the language of the National Front in France'.

the outset of the crisis, that support should be given to certain Arab countries so that they would give up the idea of unity. Western politicians and intellectuals, especially those in France and including those who have, in the past, supported Arab freedom movements, have never wanted to see in the idea of Arab unity anything other than the proof of a certain longing for the past, a reminder of the concept of imperialism, that archaic and unrealistic powerhouse for the creation of violence and fanaticism. The occupation of Kuwait was only of interest in that it demonstrated the negative nature of Arab nationalism, and above and beyond that, of the Arabs themselves. This occupation could be said to constitute the best possible illustration of the failure of Arab nationalism and a tangible proof of its demise. This helps to explain the sudden concern for the future of Kuwait, a country which had previously received no more attention that any other Arab state. Yet, the annexation of Kuwait was never considered by Saddam Hussein, or indeed by other Arab nations, as an integral element of Arab national unity, and yet it was announced in the context of conflict and military escalation, after the failure of the formation of a credible, provisional government.

The form of Arab nationalism which is the subject of incessant criticism is one which relates to the dignity and sovereignty of peoples who had been the victims of aggression for over a century, and who continue to suffer political, military and economic pressure at the hands of the world powers. It has nothing to do with the conquering nationalism of the colonizing Europe of the 19th and 20th centuries. In the Arab world there is no other choice but to support a union of countries facing similar circumstances, in order to guard against the sort of latent conflict that is inherent in the often arbitrary political divisions, in the precarious nature of these states, and in the spiritual, intellectual, and political communication between their peoples: this union is also vital to their chances for economic and social development. Until now, attempts to achieve unification have not amounted to much because the spontaneous and legitimate aspirations to freedom, whether generalized or regional—as in the Maghreb countries, for example—have not met with a favourable response on the part of the controlling powers, which are clinging to their immediate interests; these movements have been met with opposition by the often empty, so-called unitarian measures taken by governments. But there is nothing to suggest that rational methods which have been proven effective in other cases should not be successfully applied in this part of the world, in order to bring about the creation of a wider federation of Arab states. This will be of as much value and benefit to the Europeans as to the Arabs.

But whatever our personal assessment of the validity or reliability of this idea, it is quite simply immoral to further the concept of European unity, which I believe to be both positive and necessary, and yet to oppose, for whatever reason, the concept of the integration of the Arab world, whose peoples share a common culture and, in the majority of cases, a common language and common religion. The image of an Arab state stretching from the Atlantic to the Gulf might well be a fearful prospect for the Europeans, who have been living with the spectre of decline, now reinforced by zero population growth, since the demise of their colonial empires. However, they cannot help but recognize that the Arab world exists, and that it would pose an even greater threat if, in a quarter of a century from now, when its population reaches 500 million, it were even more divided, impoverished, and disunited than it is now. If fears and traumas from the past can be overcome, it will be possible to recognize the vital interest for Europe in helping this world to find its own state of equilibrium, its own rhythm of economic and social development, and consequently, its own positive form of integration in the civilized world. If, however, through lack of any coherent form of development, the Arab world were to collapse and be plunged into anarchy and chaos, it is Europe which would bear the brunt of the cost.

The policy of division and undermining of the Arab world was successful within the context of early mercantile colonialism, based on control of raw materials in regions with little or no clear national or social structures. It is no longer valid in a united world in this present era of communication, science and technology. Such a policy, if practised today, would lead to the acceptance of the challenge systematically to destroy whole nations, in order to maintain access to raw materials. It is quite simply a policy of divide and rule. And this is what the Americans are doing in the Middle East.

As for the question of security, it cannot be denied that the Western powers are in the wrong in their unconditional support for the expansionist policies of Israel, which are responsible for never-ending conflict and a general poisoning of the atmosphere of the region. And yet, the complete and utter oppression of the Palestinians is not the sole aspect of the problem. The systematic, steady armament of the State of Israel on the one hand, coupled with the compliance of Western countries with regard to both the development of arms of mass destruction, in particular nuclear weapons, and to the strategy of preventive war which leads to raids on an almost daily basis, raids which are never censured and are always directed against Arabs deemed to pose a threat, all this constitutes a serious challenge to all these States, and to the Arab community as a whole. The strategic doctrine as defended by the Israelis and supported by the other Western powers, in particular by the United States, seems to accept that the security of Israel can only be preserved if this country of 4 million inhabitants can maintain absolute military supremacy over the whole of the Arab world with a population in excess of 200 million inhabitants. This balance of power, deemed so vital, implies nothing less than the obligation to declare war against the Arabs every time Israel, or its allies, wishes to destroy the military or economic potential of the Arab countries. This continuous state of war, which seeks to block any Arab progress, is the incarnation of strategic imbalance and it will lead directly, and inexorably, to a general situation of conflagration and, very soon, to chaos.

The security of the Arabs, a question of vital interest for each nation, cannot be allowed to remain at the mercy of an Israeli or American general; if there is to be an end to this permanent aggression against the Arabs, an aggression which involves the weakening or blocking of any economic or technological advances, it will be necessary to modify this blinkered view, which consists of only perceiving any problems of security in the Middle East in terms of the situation of the Israelis, and which confuses security with military supremacy. But security cannot be achieved in time of war, nor in the absence of peace. Under these circumstances the idea of a Greater Israel should be laid to rest, as should the Palestinian drama which constitutes the fundamental basis of Israeli policy.

Even more problematic are those alignments which lead to a need to justify this irrational policy, of which an evermore widespread, instinctive anti-arabism is a primary feature. This anti-arabism seeks to quantify the Arab identity in the most negative way possible, on the basis of individual acts or demonstrations of popular unrest at times of economic difficulty. In fact, in the wake of the withdrawal of the Soviet Union, there is a great temptation to make the Arab character seem inhuman, even satanic in nature, in order to legitimize the aggression perpetrated against the Arabs and to preserve a climate of cold war by different means, and with new players. The most biased interpretations can be justified in this way, false interpretations of events or of Arab behaviour, which go against all critical or rational sense.*

Of course I am not speaking here of the man in the street. The support of the Arab and Muslim peoples for the Iraqi

---

* A comparison of Saddam to Hitler was not only intended to show him as a threat to the whole human race, and thus to justify the refusal of any discussion or debate on the present state of colonial tension, but also indirectly to accuse millions of Arabs and Muslims of Nazi tendencies, prior to a justification of the use of weapons of mass destruction. Moreover, public opinion in the West was not misled by this strategy: according to an American survey conducted only a few weeks after the opening of hostilities, 45% of those surveyed were in favour of the use of the atomic bomb to bring an early end to the war and to reduce the number of allied casualties. In truth, what distinguishes racism from primitive fanaticism is that the former can contemplate cold-blooded murder in a most rational and efficient manner.

people, a support which had nothing to do with any implication of support for the Iraqi government, was unfairly linked, by intellectuals and political powers, to a manifestation of fanaticism, which, in the wake of the integrationist movement, has come to be seen as a fundamental element of Arab culture. In my opinion, this attitude springs from the same immoral principle which refuses to others that which is readily acceptable for oneself, in other words, the legitimacy of solidarity amongst Western powers, a solidarity which is widely used as the main justification for Europe playing a secondary political role in the anti-Iraq coalition led by the Americans. It is to be supposed that this solidarity was based on political and moral principles, whilst Arab solidarity does not enjoy the same moral basis or political rationale.* What the Arab world had feared since the outset of the crisis, has been largely confirmed—in other words, that behind the stated objectives for the liberation of Kuwait, the United States was concealing the real aim of the war, which was to achieve the annihilation—for the third time in recent history, following that of Mohammed Ali in Egypt in the middle of the 19th century, and of Nasser in the middle of the 20th century— of an attempt to create an Arab military and technological strength, which might be in a position to re-establish a balance of military strength in the face of the devastating military domination of Israel, to give the Arab world a real centre of power or internal equilibrium and to promote its integration

---

* This tends to be the view suggested by the concepts of humiliation and frustration as discussed quite widely by Jean Daniel, editor of Le Nouvel Observateur, in his editorial: 'The reason why we are fighting' to refute the claims of the Arabs. It was precisely to defend itself against critical and condemnatory Western opinion that some Arabs began to circulate the concepts of humiliation and frustration, which do not seem to correspond to the reality of the situation. The precise reasons are more positive: they involve a determination to transform relations between strategic forces and to force those world powers responsible for the situation in the Middle East to change their policies, even if the price to pay for this warning were to be very high, if no other means exist to make themselves heard and get their message across.

into the economy of the modern world. Furthermore, the destruction of the military and economic potential of Iraq was the avowed aim of President Bush from the very first day of the hostilities. Since this aim has been almost entirely achieved, Israel has now brought forward for discussion other proposals aimed at denying the Arab world access to any aspect of progress, by bringing to an abrupt end any transfer of advanced technology towards the Arab countries, whether for military or civilian purposes (which are, moreover, closely linked to one another).

Those who seek to use all available means to tarnish the image of the Arab world, even to the extent of making privileged allies of the most extreme elements of the opposite camp in order to lend credibility to the concept of a quintessentially anti-Western Arabism, do not further the interests of the West, let alone those of the Arab world. On the contrary, they pave the way for dissension, and reinforce the argument for war. The Arab concept of solidarity is no more irrational than that of any other peoples. They all give first priority to their own economic, political, and strategic interests. Their concerted actions are not motivated by some innate sense of hatred of the West, or even towards the Israelis, but run counter to those international policies of the West which are often irrational, as well as to the expansionist and determinedly colonizing policy of Israel, and to the absence of any sense of responsibility on the part of the monarchies of the Gulf. These policies are, moreover, responsible for transforming a local conflict into a crisis on a global scale, because of their desire for supremacy.

But it is in the field of development that this major problem of security is most clearly to be observed. For as well as the negative aspects of the international economic policy implemented by the industrialized countries and by the international financial institutions which are, moreover, completely devoted to the interests of the former, the military budgets of the Arab states absorb almost all capacity for income-generating investments in most of the countries involved. The inability of the Arab states to meet the Israeli challenge and the weakening of their legitimacy together reinforce the sense of instability and insecurity felt by the ruling powers, and therefore encourage the rule of military power and dictatorships. That said, the main problem affecting Arab development is the unacceptable way in which regional resources are distributed, resulting in an illogical and colonial-like drawing of frontiers according to the disastrous Sykes-Picot agreements, which are still in force. This point has to be made, even if we do not accept today the use of force to settle disputes dating from this era of the past. It is worth recalling at this point that all the territories of the Asian region of the Arab world united in 1916 to rise up against the power of the Ottoman Empire, with the aim of achieving a united and independent Arab kingdom. It is this Arab kingdom which the Franco-British alliance divided up with a ruler in order to create a scattering of small kingdoms or Emirates, their objective being to separate the oil resources from the more populated regions. In the territories which once belonged to this now-defunct kingdom there now exist thirteen independent states which are fighting over the same political sphere of influence, for the same sense of legitimacy, the same unity, and the same human and cultural community. This division into states does not make allowance for the formation of national identities in the proper sense of the word, nor for ethnic cultural or linguistic variations. It conforms to a single rationale, namely, to serve the interests of the colonial and neo-colonial powers.

Following the independence of these states, all attempts by the Arabs to convince these minor but extremely wealthy monarchies to collaborate on a joint project for economic development were obstructed by archaic regimes who administer the national wealth as if it were their own personal fortune and who, with the support and encouragement of Western military and political protection, refuse any policies of cooperation with other countries. A telling example of this has been the Kuwait problem and the establishment of a Council for Cooperation in the Gulf, from which the other Arab countries, including Iraq, were excluded. This blindly irresponsible policy is not a new cause of the outbreak of an oil war in the Gulf. Today, the need to limit the waste of oil resources, and the misappropriation of the thousands of millions of dollars which these generate, has become a question of life or death for peoples who have no other hope of escaping economic strangulation than by the use of some of this capital to develop investment within each individual country.

Arguments can always be found to condemn any act of political behaviour. But the logic of History is implacable, as is that of the relationship between forces. When there is an unjust defeat, the war which has been lost will be transformed into a prelude to further conflict, and so is never really lost.

Both the occupation and the liberation of Kuwait appeared to be a matter of secondary importance for the Arab world, without any visible goal. What mattered most was to open up the debate on certain burning issues whose resolution will determine the future of not only hundreds of millions of Arabs, but on a wider scale, of a whole section of the human race. This was how the Arabs both perceived and analysed the destruction of the military and industrial power of Iraq, which they saw as the unstated objectives of the war. It is for this reason that, contrary to what we are led to expect, it is still difficult to convince the Arabs that this destruction, which is destined to bring about an historic capitulation on their part, is also the means by which their continuing existence will be secured, their security assured and their development and democracy guaranteed. For, in the same way that security and peace are dependent on the balance of power, so democracy cannot survive without dignity. This, however, is what we are being asked to understand in this war in the Gulf, when we are told that the destruction of military and industrial might is the only way to achieve the liberation of Kuwait, to restore a state of balance of power, to guarantee the peace to solve the Palestinian problem, to work towards a greater stability, to introduce an era of democracy, and to redistribute, in a more equitable fashion, the profits of the oil-wealth. It is clear that this kind of talk is intended to dispose European public opinion to the action being taken, and to mask the determination to restore the status quo, in other words, a return to the same situation which was the cause of the original crisis.*

Here we have typical war-time propaganda intended to justify war in terms of the benefits it is expected to bring. On this occasion, further study of the proclamations of the 'free nations' during the Second World War would suffice to convince us of this. Those colonized peoples who had all been promised their freedom and independence, dignity, and prosperity, all found themselves obliged to fight long and hard for decades—the examples of Vietnam and Algeria prove this—before acceding to a limited form of independence which was often more theoretical than actual. In the meantime, the scenes of the systematic and massive destruction of Iraq give us a foretaste of this promised era of peace and prosperity.

But a new world order is still possible. It would have been all the more possible if the European Community had been able to overcome its illusions based on past grandeur and free itself from the sway of the Americans, in order to choose a strategic and historical alliance with the Arab world; instead of opting to share the dubious glory and the booty of misery, they could have participated in the overthrow of American domination and the construction of a great Mediterranean power, an echo of the Golden Age of the Mediterranean region. The issue of the Third World is no longer so popular; the problems and the bitter competition between the industrialized powers of today do not leave any room for the accomplishment of the dream of a coherent plan of development on a global or even regional scale. But if we are unable to come up with a real aid to development, let us at least try not to favour a policy of division. It goes without saying that I am thinking here of the Arab world, to

---

* 'Is this a just war?', asks the biographer Jean Lacouture, who then proceeds to reply: 'Indeed it is, if by the use of cruel force, almost as cruel as those acts of aggression which led to the American sheriff securing a mandate to intervene, the liberation of Kuwait could lead to the initiation of discussion on other questions in the Middle East, including the problems of the Palestinians, the Lebanese, and the Kurds'.

which Nature has granted certain resources which are being systematically subverted, due to the selfishness of the Sheiks, the irresponsibility of dictators, and with the help of certain industrial powers intent on furthering their own interests by this aid.

Whatever the circumstances, if there were to be no prospect of a genuine awareness of the seriousness of the economic, political, and social situation in the Third World, and if a courageous attempt to overcome vested interests in order to permit a real move towards negotiations between all nations were not to be made in time to bring some real order into the administration of questions of global importance, then the Gulf war will lead inexorably to a widespread economic battle for the control of scarce resources, in which both larger and smaller powers will be involved. In this case, we will remember the Gulf war as a dress-rehearsal prior to the era of large-scale conflicts, which will radically modify the global balance of power, on a shorter time scale than we perhaps expect, especially in the Mediterranean basin. The Western world is likely to come out of this final world struggle considerably weakened and with diminished political and economic power; it would have to face the irresistible ascension, both morally and materially, of those poorer countries who do not really have anything left to lose.

Politics and International Law

Monique Chemillier-Gendreau*

Since August 1990, international legal experts have been experiencing a sense of unease. Politicians and the leaders of international institutions have taken over from the former their traditional sphere of influence, so that by their cunning and by some deplorable sleight of hand, these latter have tried to pass off as an act of international justice what amounts, in fact, to taking the law into their own hands. The credulous public, their critical faculties dulled by a daily diet of dreary media dispatches, went so far as to applaud this manoeuvre. International legal experts were left speechless with amazement. My comments are intended to redress their inability to reply, through the development of a three-part analysis.

• the United Nations charter is an instrument for peace which should, technically speaking, afford real possibilities for guaranteeing an international legal system;

• this charter has been violated in various ways; during the present crisis, it has been manipulated or openly disregarded, and this has led to the Gulf War;

• however, during the current crisis, political manoeuvres have only been able to get the better of the law by invoking that same law. This not only discredits the United Nations and the peace-keeping mission entrusted to them, which requires them to guarantee the peace through observation of the law, bu

* Professor of Law at the University of Paris VII.

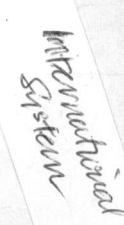

points to a vitally important need, in the very near future, for an international legal system.

This is, in truth, one of the aspects of the state of paradox which currently prevails.

* * *

The virtues and merits of the United Nations Charter should not be underestimated. Moreover, the quality of the overall extent of its provisions should not be surprising. Its authors learned from the negative experience of the League of Nations. The Second World War had given those politicians and legal experts who came together, first at Dumbarton Oaks and then in San Francisco, the opportunity to reflect on the value of peace and on the means to be pursued in an attempt to ensure its continuing existence.

The values upheld by the peoples of the United Nations are set forth in the Preamble.

Peace, and the means for ensuring peace (protection of Human Rights, equality, justice, liberty, tolerance, friendly relations, cooperation) and their common objectives. The objective of peace was first enshrined in a radically innovative statute, in 1945, in which Member States were forbidden to have recourse to force (article 2, para. 4).

An essentially positive quality, peace constitutes the underlying mission of the institution as an entity. All of its members are obliged to contribute to the upholding and implementation of its Charter. But two bodies have a more specific role, one more so than the other: the Security Council and the General Assembly.

The Security Council is invested with primary responsibility in this domain, and is mandated to act by all the members (article 24).

Firstly, this mandate requires the peaceful settlement of disputes (chapter VI). It comprises a series of long and detailed measures by means of which, in a determined effort for peace, the statute provides for an objective body (i.e. a third party to those parties governed by their respective and subjective views at the time of a given dispute) which will attempt to identify the cause of the dispute, to bring the two parties involved to state their respective points of view, to clear up any misunderstandings, and to cut down to size any excessive ambitions or claims.

As the possibility of these provisions being inadequate cannot be ruled out, it is essential to make provision for a response to the following question: what would happen if one of the Member States were to violate the new law and use force against another Member State?

It is here that we can see the inevitable necessity of a means of regulations or sanctions, which could only be administered by the institution itself. According to this logic, if there were a threat to the peace, a violation of the peace or an act of aggression, the Security Council has at its disposal the possibilities afforded by Chapter VII:

• it has those full powers on which all legal initiatives are based, and its first task is to identify any violation of the law;

• it can then decide on non-military measures (economic or diplomatic) (article 41);

• and finally, but only then, if these measures prove inadequate or are shown to be so, the Security Council has at its disposal the overwhelming power to undertake, by deployment of air, land or sea forces, any action it may consider necessary to maintain or restore peace and international security (article 42).

The Security Council exercises all these responsibilities according to the procedures regulating voting, as laid down in article 27: that is, there has to be an assenting vote by nine of its members, including the votes of all permanent members.

Thus these latter (the veto powers) each have the veto. But since the Council comprises 15 members, the 10 non-permanent members still have the power of veto, even if they cannot exercise it on an individual basis, provided that at least 7 of them want to exercise this vote. In this way, the five permanent members cannot muster the required majority, even if they all unite and align with the three remaining members. In other words, the non-permanent members are not totally deprived of power. This is the mechanism by which the Security Council is given primary responsibility for upholding the peace.

However, the General Assembly is not left completely out of the picture. Articles 10 and 11 give it such powers as to make its scope more general, less clearly-defined, and more especially, subordinated to those of the Security Council (article 12). It has the right to discuss any question relating to the upholding of peace, and on these matters it has the power to make recommendations. It does not have any power to enforce any actions.

Two further comments on the role of the General Assembly are necessary, however: *1.* on any given matter, this role is suspended to some extent for as long as the Security Council is fulfilling those responsibilities devolved to it. But once the Security Council ceases to fulfil that function, then the General Assembly resumes its powers on questions relating to the keeping of the peace (article 12, interpretation by negative inference); *2.* to this must be added a reminder of the customary extension of the role of the General Assembly, instituted in 1950 by the resolution on the Union for the keeping of the peace (also called the Dean Acheson resolution). It must also be noted that when the Security Council is prevented, by the power of veto, from fulfilling its primary responsibility, the General Assembly has the right to take over its role.

The authorization of this right lies in the inability of the Security Council to function. Although any breakdown has, for many years, been due to a blocking by veto, any breakdown of the functioning of the Security Council for any other reason can lead to the same consequences: that is, the devolving on to the General Assembly of the responsibility for keeping the peace. The mechanism for doing this requires the Assembly to meet in extraordinary session (article 20).

To conclude this brief summary of the way in which the United Nations functions, mention should be made of the International Court of Justice, the legal body of the United Nations, which completes the picture and contributes to ensuring the peace, either by its advice, or by jurisdictional settlement of

legal disputes referred to it. This overview of the institution*
shows it to comprise an as yet embryonic, but already relatively
well-organized, system of legal regulation of the relations between
Member States.

*   *   *

The peace-keeping role of the United Nations has long been
neglected because social regulation was enforced purely and
simply by a balance of fear. A certain degree of political self-
effacement on the part of the Soviet Union, and the end to the
clash of power-blocs brought about by the policies of Gorbachev,
have since disrupted this state of affairs. Intervention by the
United Nations has once again become evident in the Gulf crisis.
If this crisis has degenerated into a war, it is because of the non-
observance of the provisions of the Charter.

When we consider the invasion and annexation of Kuwait,
how can we not support the enforcement of Chapter VII of the
Charter? The fact that it had not been previously used to settle
other, similar cases (which could still, however, be dealt with in
the same way) was not in itself a reason for continuing non-
observance of the law. And so we cannot but approve the view
of the Iraqi invasion as a violation of the peace on the basis of
article 39† and economic sanctions (article 4) as an acceptable
initial measure. Thus far, and if nothing of a dubious nature had
been detected immediately following the first movements of
censure, there would be nothing to criticize.

But preparations for war were going on at the same time, on
an unlawful basis. The sequence of events seemed to sanction
the rejection of any reference to the legal statute (except through
the voice of the media):

● the failure of the embargo was not established before pro-

* Refer to the article by article Commentary on the Charter by Jean-Pierre
Cot and Alain Pellet. Economica-Bruylant, Paris, 1985.

† Refer to the publication on this important matter of the authority and
power of the Security Council by Jean Combacau. *The authority of sanction of
the United Nations.* pp. 108 ff. Pedone, Bordeaux, 1974.

gressing to the use of military intervention (violation of article 42);

• the Committee of the Chiefs of Staff did not meet and was not responsible for the strategic direction of all the armed forces (violation of article 47);

• the Security Council itself did not draw up the plans for the deployment of the armed forces (violation of article 46).

There is no point in entering into an argument over the interpretation of these texts; the rules governing the interpretation of treaties are well known.*

The ban on the use of force is a cardinal principle of the legal system founded by the Charter. When the Security Council authorized the Member States to use force as a means of sanction, it was in fact an exception to this principle. The texts give strict guidelines. They are, moreover, sufficiently clear to permit interpretation according to 'the commonly understood meaning of the terms'. If any element of doubt were to creep in regarding an article, there should be no hesitation: recourse should be made to what specialists call a teleological interpretation, which interprets words in conformity with the overall sense of the text.

It is certainly true that the use of force should be strictly adapted to the objective of the sanction and that in no way should it degenerate, in its turn, into that scourge of war against which 'we, the people of the United Nations, have resolved to protect future generations . . .'. In this spirit, the control exercised by the Security Council over military plans is of prime importance. The special agreements provided for in article 43 were never concluded, as we know. But it was the responsibility of the Council, once the decision was taken to have recourse to military intervention, to insist on a speedy conclusion of these agreements, which means proceeding to the immediate enforcement of article 46—and there is nothing to prevent this. It is for this reason that the main body of the UN did not fulfil the functions delegated to it by the Charter. The General Assembly did not make an

---

* They are described in articles 31 ff. of the Vienna Convention on Treaty Law of 29 May, 1969.

issue of this, did not demand a meeting, and did not use the powers which it holds under established usage according to the Acheson article. Nor did it refer the legal aspects of the problem to the International Court. International law, however discredited by this, is still even more necessary than ever.

* * *

In a purely realistic assessment of the situation, analysts would be forgiven for giving way to a deeply pessimistic view and for wondering how the UN, and the international order it has a mandate to establish, could manage to recover from such a failure. Certain factors lead nonetheless to the view that this crisis, over and above all the negative effects which will be deep-rooted and long-lasting, will have brought to light the unavoidable necessity for a genuine recourse to international law.

Modern societies are essentially politically-motivated, and in this respect international society functions on the same lines as a society on a national level. The law is an instrument of regulation subordinated to the power of the state, in certain cases even controlled by it. But the law, by its very structure (and by what it dictates through the standards it establishes) can never be entirely separate from a form of justice based on a moral code. There thus exists both *what the law says*, and *what interpretation of the law is made*. The first has regard to representation, and so to values. The second relates to actual practice. This latter may express some counter-values. This is the current situation in international law. The legal mechanisms of the Charter, by the values which it preaches, are in direct opposition to those which are secretly undermining Western society. This much has become obvious in recent months.

It is worth recalling, in a close look at the texts, the values upheld by the Charter:

To save succeeding generations from the scourge of war . . .
To practise tolerance . . .
To accept principles and ensure, by the acceptance of the

institution of measures to ensure that armed force shall not be used, save in the common interest . . .

To bring about by peaceful means, and in conformity with the principles of justice and international law, the adjustment or settlement of international disputes or situations, which might lead to a breach of the peace . . .

To build relations based on the respect for the principle of equal rights and self-determination of peoples (Article 1(2)) . . .

To employ international machinery for the promotion of the economic and social advancement of all peoples . . . and Article 2(1) states that the United Nations is based on the principle of the sovereign equality of all its members.

This is surely the reflection, on an international level, of those values enshrined in the West, which are the rational values of democracy. The judgement of Reason would have to lead both individuals and nations to a state of equilibrium based on the respect of all men, in which the law assures the equality of each individual.

Without a doubt, there has never been, in the history of the United Nations, a time when the principal player in world society (i.e. the United States and its allies) have behaved in a manner so far removed from that which these principles would lead one to expect.

In the competitive world market, with the economic policy of liberalism forced upon it, there has for many years existed a gap between the original principles and values of the Charter and attempts to apply these in real-life situations. If political decolonization has been, from this aspect, a very positive achievement on the part of the United Nations, it has become more and more bogged down since the 1960s. Economic decolonization has run its course, and has met its demise in the flowing rhetoric of the new international economic order. For the past 10 years the whole world has watched with amazement as the West, China and their allies have allowed the seat for the representative of Cambodia at the UN to be occupied by the Khmer Rouge, those cynical and uncensured perpetrators of recognized crimes against humanity who are responsible for the

Cambodian genocide. Disarmament, an essential condition for peace, did not become what it should have: i.e. the main objective of the organization.

Entangling the smaller or weaker nations in a net of debt, the countries of the West, like skillful predators, have encouraged the rule of these States by men whose co-operation could be relied upon because it had been bought. On the whole, these latter did not betray their masters on the question of this war; the betrayal of their peoples is another matter.

They stood for the counter values of the world against those original values of the Charter. International democracy could not withstand the challenge. Sovereign equality has never been a less uniformly distributed privilege. Resembling a bone to be fought over, this equality should not, under any circumstances, enable any of those who enjoy it, if not members of the original Club, to exercise in any way any shred of power which does not come under the jurisdiction of their masters.

Does a heavily-armed Saddam Hussein represent a danger? That is an indisputable fact. But an excessively over-armed George Bush is even more dangerous! This argument has not met with general acclaim and the general tendency seems to reverse the argument and credit American armament with a protective role.

Keeping a watch on all fronts, the United States and its 'allies' (whether this means the European countries, of which its closest supporter is the faithful United Kingdom, or the Arab countries, or those of the Third World led by governments whose willingness to oblige is well-known) make sure that they exercise strict control over the maintenance of these conditions of inequality, including a control of all sources of raw materials, all financial and market systems and every arms purchase.

Those so-called intermediary powers are kept under close surveillance and none of them can undergo any state of growth, especially in the region of the Middle East where they seek to maintain the security of Israel, by a great contradiction in terms, through the weakness of the Arab nations and not by the solution of the Palestinian problem. This solution, although the most important factor in the question of peace in the region, has been the subject of indefinite procrastination. The current failure of the United Nations is also due to the fact of its having produced so many unenforced resolutions on the subject. To rectify this would require a strict enforcement of the law with regard to Israel.

If an excessively obvious inequality in the political and military treatment of nations is seen to corrupt international society, it is still those aspects of culture and religion which are indisputably the most difficult to reconcile from the point of view of a truly international law. Much has been said and written on this point since the start of this war. Conflict between North and South, a split between West and East, an inability at the centre of this dominant ideology to accept the Other with all his differences. Although it has become quite commonplace, the subject deserves some consideration.

The identification of a very large section of the Arab peoples, and also of the peoples of the Third World, with the Iraqi government and its leader, whilst regrettable, is inevitable, and is linked to a rather confused but understandable perception of the way in which these latter have been manipulated by the Western powers over the past ten years.

Having carefully built up his country's arms, Saddam Hussein, this leader of a secular Arab government, was supported by a large coalition of Western states which had allowed him to make war on Iran, a war he called the Islamic Revolution. When this war drew to an end, he was supposed to give back the valuable military gadgets, especially since this versatile man, once in possession of them, had begun to make dangerous threats to use them in the name of Islam, which for the West was seen as a rhetorical figure for the Devil. This violation of international law, which in itself should attract condemnation and chastisement, also produced consequences which went beyond any legally-enforced sanctions supported by military power.

Of all the issues at stake which combined to reinforce each other in the build up to war, that of the simple fact of domination by the West will appear, for a long time to come, as the one with the most negative impact. Its very presence in the debate leads any reflections towards a series of decisive questions.

Some would like to press forward and talk of a world government, for which there do not exist as yet any basic principles, nor have any of the conditions for its existence been drawn up. It is clear to see that America dreams of leading the world as it joins battles rendered less difficult by the absence of its main adversary, and in which its own moral stance is not questioned. There are few nations who would be prepared to give open encouragement and legal support to this dream.

The current state of affairs, instigated in 1945, and on which the war in the Gulf should not be allowed to close a chapter, is that of the institution and reinforcement of an international legal system (constituting not a mere formality but a clearly identifiable element of a world-wide government). This order should be the harbinger of peace for the future, and should devise an acceptable role for each nation, according to its individual characteristics, within the framework of a genuine state of equality before the law. All nations should perceive this order as one to be respected by each individual nation.

What can be done to avoid the possibility of the Third World countries rejecting this international legal order as one which appears to be manipulated to their disadvantage? Dare we say that since decolonization, or rather, since the failure of the new international economic order (the 1960s was a time when legal experts and those in authority in the new states showed a definite penchant for observance of the law) the very nature of the constitution meant that this international system, with its institutions, its relative standardization, its conciliation tribunals, and its financial systems, became alienated from these countries, so that they saw themselves as victims rather than as participants or beneficiaries?

This is due to two factors: *1.* Because this very complex legal system, comprehensible only to accredited experts in the field, only enshrines a feeble imitation of the strong, positive, universal values proclaimed in the Charter. Close encounters with this system have left those involved with a sense of bitterness. *2.* The second reason is that even if one could imagine that this legal system were devised in such a way as to put into practice those principles as proclaimed, it would still be expressed in certain terms, which would not be common to the different cultures involved, but only those of one single culture, the West's.

This is a legal system which has, over the centuries, tried (and I mean tried) to purge itself of any reference to religious or sacred concepts; to cease to be based on a motivating principle which cannot be demonstrated, and on the contrary, to build its foundations on a rational and specific set of criteria. These should not be dictated by an external force (God) but based on the irrefutable logic of the only possible rationale; the system should therefore be seen to represent the common good. Thus, even if several implied criteria seem to be drawn from religious traditions,* the proposed international legal order can defend its claim to rationality. And so those cultures whose legal systems enshrine a sizeable general element of religious principles cannot be integrated into this order, but are left by the wayside, either excluded or self-excluding.

The problem is not inconsequential. Whether we look at states from the Muslim world, and this includes all the Islamic states, or the State of Israel, or India, or many others, these are all states which have not adopted a form of secular government which could facilitate dialogue and communication within some kind of common framework of reference.

Should these states be encouraged to develop this form of government? Would it not be more desirable to review very carefully the laws and the way in which they are formulated, in order to adapt their more admirable elements to some form of language which could be understood by all, taking into account all the differences which currently exist.

These are the difficult questions which the system of international law will have to answer in the period which lies ahead.

* See Pierre Legendre, Le désir politique de Dieu. Paris. Fayard, 1988.

The Ayatollah of the West. How Hans Magnus Enzensberger became a Satanist

*Günther Nenning**

In Germany, far more than in Britain, the Gulf War divided the intellectuals. The writer Hans Magnus Enzensberger, well known for his radical stance on social and cultural issues, surprised many by coming out on the side of those who defended the war. His views were published in France by the newspaper *Libération* and found an equally large echo in Italy and here in Britain. Now we offer the other side of the argument, in the form of a response to Enzensberger's philippic from Günther Nenning, himself a writer of considerable renown. It was originally published in *Die Zeit*.

I mourn the passing of Hans Magnus Enzensberger, victim of the Gulf war. Born 1929 in the Allgau, he grew up in Nuremberg amidst the air raids. At 16 a member of Hitler's *Volkssturm*, he soon became an intellectual of the left, an important German poet and (if it's possible for a German) a good revolutionary. The first love affair is always the best and revolution is like a first love. In the first phase, everything seems more beautiful—flowers, animals, and even people—or, at least, those deemed intelligent enough to join in! The third phase of the revolution (let's skip the second phase, the obligatory bloodbath, since there wasn't one in the revolution of 1968) is also very interesting. The revolutionaries begin to lose their way, straying in to the most unlikely of places. Hans Magnus Enzensberger, for example,

* German author.

the most enlightened of all the luminaries of 1968, has become a Satanist.

Thus, in *Der Spiegel* (No. 6, 1991) we find him on the trail of the 'enemy of the human race'. And hardly has he found this being, he immediately begins to draw comparisons. His judgement is merciless and absolute: Saddam equals Hitler. George Bush, it is true, has already made this comparison—but I'm no anti-American who would deny the President such intellectual assistance. Enzensberger, 'wants to try and show that the portrayal of Saddam Hussein as a new Hitler is neither a journalistic metaphor nor a propagandistic exaggeration but nothing more than the essential truth.' Saddam, you see, is 'not just intent on suppressing a nation, dominating it, exploiting it and enjoying for as long as possible the pleasure afforded by such an enterprise; his real enemy is the world. His primary motive force is pure aggression. . . . For himself, he asks only the privilege of being the last to die. The parallel to Hitler is obvious. . . . It is therefore not to demonize him, but simply to describe the facts that we call him what he is: an enemy of the human race.' Seven times on three printed pages Enzensberger describes Saddam in this way. Beyond such repetition, however, Enzensberger offers precious little by way of proof. But perhaps that isn't the point. The Gulf war, involving as it does the most advanced machinery of destruction in the history of warfare, has made us uneasy. We need a clear and simple picture of the enemy—and here it is. The 'enemy of the human race' is to blame for everything. Everything can be off-loaded on to him (including bombs). A simple message to hold on to.

Thus, the warring parties in the Gulf are mirror images of each other, insofar as the oil-polluted Gulf reflects anything any more. Both sides see their opponents as the devil. Enzensberger is the Ayatollah of the West.

But it wasn't Hitler who made Hitler. It is we who are to blame for not having stopped him in time. Saddam is not to blame for the fact that we didn't stop him in time either. The rise of dictators is not irresistible. Enzensberger, however, chooses to believe in the devil. For him, the 'enemy of the human race' is unstoppable. 'No conceivable policy, no matter how clever or carefully planned, can deal with such an enemy.'

Comrades, give up. If the devil won't play ball, there ain't nothing you can do. Thus, Enzensberger, Satan's new troubadour. No, the world enemy Hitler couldn't have been stopped. Not even if the democrats had made a genuine, viable democracy with which one could really identify. Not even if the democrats opposing Hitler had held together, instead of arguing with each other. Not even with a couple of divisions of the French army, then the strongest in Europe, at the point when Hitler marched into the Rhineland in 1936, backed only by a puny force. Not even in 1938, when Austria called for help from the Western democracies and they merely shrugged their shoulders in return. Not even in 1939, when Hitler was fully occupied in Poland and the Allies could have caught him from behind.

Oh, Enzensberger, in better days, in the review *Kursbuch* of 1965, you were such an insightful analyst and historian of the old, the new, and the third worlds. And now here you are bending your knee before the great Satan Saddam. Yet if the western democracies hadn't equipped him with the most up-to-date weaponry (so that he could fight the great Satan Khomeni), Saddam would never have been anything more than a miserable little dictator. He wouldn't have become the hero of the Arab masses either if the western democracies had used the 45 years since the end of World War II to create their 'new world order', not with bombs and grenades, but by reducing the disparities between rich and poor.

But why am I talking? Enzensberger has got Satan on the brain. Nothing and no one is to be allowed to dislodge this Satan. Certainly not *das Volk*, the people. Yet it is the people who continually, and often unexpectedly, haul down the great Satans from their thrones, though often as not only to find themselves conned into accepting new ones.

I have often had the suspicion that left-wingers can't actually stand the people. The people, you see, refuse to do what they are told. And, indeed, Enzensberger puts the people in the dock as principal defendants alongside the two enemies of the human

race. 'A Hitler or a Saddam can arrive on the historical stage',
he tells us, 'only if a whole people wishes them to do so . . . The
Germans were the Iraqis of 1938–45 . . . What so attracted the
Germans was not just the licence to kill, but even more, the
chance of being killed themselves. Today, with equal fervour,
millions of Arabs express the wish to die for Saddam.'

Thus, escorted by Satan, Enzensberger goes down to the
Iraqis in the bunkers, some of them buried alive, some still
surviving, and calls out: na, na, serves you right, you were the
ones who were so keen to die. And, with the devil at his elbow,
Enzensberger also knows *why* the enemy of the human race
manages to excite such fervour among his imbecilic people: 'Why
does he find so many followers, yearning for Armageddon? The
answer lies in a long history of perceived national humiliation
which has undermined the masses' self-esteem.' They've got
something seriously wrong with them, these masses of the Third
World. They yearn—somehow Enzensberger just *knows* this—
not for a decent life or anything like that, no, its Armageddon
or nothing. Out of the misery of the South (which actually ought
to prompt solidarity and neighbourly love), Enzensberger cobbles
together his accusations of devil-worship.

Some Islamic sects believe not in one God and one devil but
in one God and two devils. That's much more useful than
Enzensberger's Mono-Satanism. Because then the tortured Iraqi
people could have two devils to curse, namely Bush and Saddam.
To learn from history is to learn to speak in the conditionl tense.
If you get to nascent Satans early enough, then you can clip their
horns without too much trouble. But that sort of trifling lesson
doesn't provide enough nourishment for a Satanist. Instead,
Enzensberger gorges himself on absolutes. 'In the end, the enemy
of the human race always gets what he wants, namely, war . . .
removing Hitler cost the lives of countless millions. The price
for removing Saddam Hussein off the face of the globe will be
astronomical.'

The enlightened hope of learning from past mistakes so as to
avoid them in the future—history as learning process—is indeed
pale beer compared with Enzensberger's powerful Armageddon

ale. It is true that, after his irresistible rise to power, the enemy
of the human race *will* be rubbed out. But the US high-tech
machine is also erasing an astronomical number of innocents in
the process. Moreover, the whole enterprise will probably achieve
nothing anyway. With nihilistic gusto, Enzensberger's already
serving up the next round of his Armageddon brew. 'Perhaps',
he writes, the great Satan Saddam 'will narrowly fail to unleash
the nuclear war to which he aspires . . . his successors, however,
will surely succeed . . . on the Indian subcontinent and in the
Soviet Union the nuclear arsenal is ready and waiting'.

Isn't there a nuclear arsenal missing there? Oh, yes, the eight
thousand or so atomic bomblets belonging to the USA. Of
course, they're not for Satan's use but to create a new world
order. Yet Enzensberger doesn't have much time for this new
world order. Instead he plays a sort of post-modern version of
the witches in Macbeth. Visions appear—of one enemy of the
human race after another. 'Where Hitler and Saddam failed, in
attaining the final victory, or rather achieving the final solution,
their heirs may succeed.'

I prefer even the Pope to Enzensberger. 'War is not the way
to solve conflicts', pronounced the old reactionary apropos the
Gulf War. That's easy to say, of course, but better saying that
than this talk of the enemy of the human race. Enzensberger is
only a demi-Ayatollah. He preaches about the great Satan, but
not the victory of good over evil that's supposed to go with it.
It was Karl Kraus, that naive pacifist, who described how even
great poets fall for the attractions of war. In his 'Sinking of the
Titanic' (1978), Enzensberger developed the following 'theoretical model of learning':

> Here you have
> a big box
> with the inscription:
> box.
> When you open it
> you find within
> a box
> with the inscription:

box . . .
And so on . . .
It is a box
that exists
only in your imagination.
A completely empty
box.

With the inscription Enzensberger. We'll have to put it away in
the attic. It's a shame, because right now we could really do with
boxes that have got something in them.

In better days, Enzensberger produced a marvellous descrip-
tion (in *The Short Summer of Anarchy* in 1972) of what it is to be
a full-blooded revolutionary, in other words, what Enzensberger
himself wanted to be: 'They're never careless or superficial in
their approach to things . . . but they're not melancholics
either . . . they have the dignity of people who have never given
in . . . they are incorruptible . . . they are not worn out has-
beens . . . their defeats have not made them defeatists.' And yet
here he is presenting the world to us—this world that so cries
out for change—as an irresistible succession of irresistible Satans.
Superficial, melancholy, worn out, and defeatist.

The Gulf War: What Has Changed

*Robert Bistolfi**

Régis Debray said: 'When the flag is unfurled, all reason flies away with the notes of the bugle call.' It has indeed been difficult to retain one's head with the army trumpets blaring, whilst on the ground things have been happening at an ever increasing pace, information has been patchy and manipulated, and the real war aims became evident only late in the day. Everything invited caution, because the objective basis of any forward-looking analysis was still too uncertain.

It is impossible to predict today the political restructuring of tomorrow in the Near and Middle East and more generally in the Arab-Muslim world. Nevertheless, some observations can be made now. Without doubt, irreversible changes have taken place since 2 August 1990 and especially since 15 January 1991 and the start of military operations. These changes concern not only the future of Israel in the region, but also the self-perception of the Arab world as a whole (the 'Arab nation'), the present relevance of the 'Mediterranean project' and the nature of the links between France and Maghreb countries.

The relationship between France and the Arab world, and more generally between Europe and the Arab world, has undergone a radical change. Some would argue that harsh reality (economic dependence, the obligations posed by the neighbouring countries) will revive the old patterns, once the emotion of the Arab masses which we see now has subsided.

* Institut du Monde Arabe, Paris.

This argument overlooks the fact that fundamental collective transformations are based not only—and not in the first instance—on material arithmetic, whatever the constraints it imposes, but on collective awareness and symbolic breaks. In this respect, the gulf war will have caused several symbolic breaks, the extent of which have not yet been fully measured. The questions uncovered by the war often take on the appearance of paradoxes. Even though the military defeat of Iraq will considerably strengthen Israel's security, has not the war rendered Israel's long-term integration in the region and its acceptance by the Arab world, in short its very existence, uncertain? And, whilst the Arab states confront each other militarily for the first time and the divisions between them, which go beyond even the bilateral crises which used to bring them into conflict, are deeper and more serious than those which formed around President Anwar Sadat's decision to support the Camp David process, has not the war revealed the cohesion of the substratum within the 'Arab nation' (we shall return to this term later) and the strength and durability of the emotion felt by hundreds of millions of people who ensure its survival, in spite of the diversity of political regimes and the collective humiliation of defeat, and who tomorrow may enable it to have an organized political expression?

Israel

The first Scud to hit Israel was above all a political Scud. The missile made up for its lack of technical precision by causing terrible political fall-out, in that it may have wiped out decades of work aimed at establishing the Jewish state in an Arab world on which it had once been imposed. The long and difficult road to recognition of Israel by the Arab states—marked by Camp David, the Fez Plan, the Declaration of the Algiers-based Palestinian National Council—is in the forefront of everyone's mind. Far-right governments in Israel have never repaid the compliment; they have not even tried to implement the cautious measures in the Camp David agreement relating to the 'occupied territories'. Since the Intifada, their refusal to negotiate with the PLO has closed the door to any alternative to brutal repression.

The clever manoeuvres of the 'Shamir Plan' cannot hide the fact that Israel's security is always approached from the military point of view, never from the starting-point that global dialogue might be possible. This almost exclusively military approach to security makes sanctuarization of national territory, which is admittedly quite understandable given the exiguity of Israel's position, inevitable. It also makes it necessary to preserve at all costs weapons superiority, which the Americans are committed to ensuring and which caused President Hafez Assad to wear himself out in an attempt to establish strategic parity. Finally, it means a policy of deterrence based on preventive actions and reprisals on a massive scale, such as the destruction of the Osirik reactor, numerous incursions into Lebanon, and a raid on Tunis.

Against this policy, there are the opinions of Arab populations outraged by feelings of injustice and helplessness: the injustice of the fate dished out to the Palestinians, helplessness in the face of Israeli arrogance and the cynical use made of the Palestinian cause by numerous Arab regimes whose chief aim is to divert internal demands for democracy towards an external enemy. Contrary to what too many Western commentators, who can only see these well-informed and politically aware Arab publics through the memory of the fields of boots left behind in the Sinai by the retreating Egyptians in 1967, trot out, their feelings are of revolt and anger rather than humiliation.

This then, is the political and psychological ground on which the first Scud hit Tel Aviv on 18 January; that 'dodgy firecracker' showed that Israel was not protected forever against Arab weapons. The 'restraint' for which Israel was praised only served to underline the point: Israel's strength is due to massive support from the West, mainly the USA, at decisive moments. But the invincibility given by Western support now appears in all its true fragility. This vulnerability is real in the long term perspective, beyond the immediate effects of Iraq's defeat. Patriot anti-war missiles were shown to be less than 100% effective, so what will happen in the future? The support of European states, kept alive by a collective feeling of guilt, is now less certain and will be increasingly undermined as time goes on. Even the USA is not free from social changes and internal politics which could diminish the influence of the pro-Israeli lobby. And, in the long run, demographic trends will impose the iron law of numbers, despite the influx of Soviet Jews.

Although these facts may be incomplete and insufficiently weighted, they are nonetheless perceived by the peoples of the Arab world. Deep down, does not each Arab citizen now feel that, having been endlessly forced to keep giving proof of their recognition of Israel's right to existence, Arabs henceforth have the right to demand proof from Israel that it is not just a foreign bridge-head in the Arab world—proof which, in their opinion, Israel has never been willing to give? For now they are sure that, if all else fails, they will one day—in ten years, in twenty years— be able to impose on Israel what it has never wanted to concede through negotiation and compromise.

If anything, we need to be careful that this reassessment of the situation does not go beyond simply restoring Arab self-confidence and risk undoing the painful steps taken towards acceptance of Israel. That is what the Gulf war has also shown: in the long term, Israel's survival is less certain than it was before a ramshackle Scud caused one person in Tel Aviv to die of a heart attack.

The 'Arab nation'

Words carry with them a culture and a history; they are traps when they claim to express directly a reality which has its roots in a different culture: thus *al-Oumma al-Arabiyya* which is translated in over-simplified form as 'Arab nation'. The 'Arab nation' is an entity whose reality tends to be denied by Western experts, deliberately, because its potentialities worry them and because it does not fit into the simplistic categories of Western political and institutional approaches based largely on the nation-state. Or they tend to see it as a component with only emotional substance, which was used by populist ideologies such as Nasserism but came up against the diverse reality of the constituent Arab states.

The term 'Arab nation' can be retained, since its use is now well established, but it must always be made clear that the term designates a reality other than the state, which we in the West tend to link with nation. In fact, in France, for example, the almost complete equation of the concepts of nation and nation-state is the result of an historical evolution which itself has been over-simplified; in the old sense of the word, 'nation' signified a societal grouping with a common language, territorial establishment and specific cultural traits which together, usually in the absence of any political and institutional framework, formed the basis for a lasting identity.

Al-Oumma al-Arabiyya designates a 'community for being', a more complex reality than the simple concept of 'nation-state' and also more able to adapt to the ups and downs of history, because it is held together by a homogeneous culture, of which religion is a strong and cohesive element, but not the only one. Viewed in this light, the long list of unsuccessful attempts at unification of constituent Arab states does not deserve the irony heaped on it by Western commentators. Neither does it justify the view, based on the ephemeral nature of alliances and the crazy geometry of official liaisons between Arab states, that *Al-Oumma al-Arabiyya* hides an illusion which is easily manipulated by the political regime of the day. Today, when the Arab states are more than ever divided among themselves, there is a greater than ever temptation to think that references to the Arab nation are mere rhetoric which has lost all power of political mobilization. In other words, that we are at the end of a long process similar to that which in Europe, at the end of the Roman empire and with the dispersion of the Christian order, saw the rise of nations with increasingly divergent identities and trajectories.

We do not have the space here to embark on an analysis of the dialectical relationship which in the Arab world never separated assertions of autonomy from a permanent renewal of the old forces of cohesion. What is important, although the apparent division of Arab peoples in the two camps of the Gulf War obscured it and future settling of scores under the gaze of the victors will continue to conceal it, is the great sense of unity which mobilized public opinion in all Arab lands in support of the Iraqi people. Admittedly, this mobilization was encouraged in some places by circumstantial factors, which would need to be analysed. It must also be said that public opinion in the West, ill-informed and misunderstanding the meaning of this support, saw it only as the confirmation of the congenital fickleness and fanaticism of the Arab peoples and their unerring capacity for choosing mediocre heroes.

This inadequate and caricatural analysis is shared by many in the West, even by so-called orientalists. They could be in for a surprise: it has perhaps escaped people's attention that it is in the Arab countries—the Maghreb countries, Jordan, Yemen— where democracy and freedom of expression have made the most significant progress in recent years that support for the Iraqi people and criticism of Western intervention were strongest. Everything indicates that ordinary people and intellectuals alike feel the same way whether they live in Damascus or Cairo, Nouakchott or Aden, regardless of different choices of government: more than humiliation (visible, and unbearable to watch, on the faces of the starved Iraqi soldiers paraded obscenely in front of the television cameras before the eyes of the victorious GIs) they feel revolt against an international law which works imperfectly, selective compassion (how many Arab children must die in order to get the same emotional response from the West as to the death of an Israeli?), general hypocrisy, and an ignorance and disregard for other cultures which are staggering in the West: to think that, in an era of world-wide media communication, commentators can make 'slips' like that of the television commentator who spoke of 'the civilized world and the Arab world'!

The Arab world is divided, brought low by defeat. As far as Arab public opinion can see, Iraq's double defeat, military and political, the even more uncertain fate of the Palestinians, the 'rewards' which will be dished out to the Arab states which participated in the coalition, and Israel's new-found confidence all mean a cloudy horizon. In this context, popular feeling, fuelled by a sense of stalemate, could get out of control.

Beyond the confusion which will no doubt prevail in the immediate future, however, the Arab nation will probably emerge strengthened from the ordeal. There is the paradox: a real community only tests its cohesiveness in the face of adversity, and in the longer term *al-Oumma al-Arabiyya* will continue to confirm its existence as a community of destiny. Confronted by the outside, confined by others in their 'otherness', the Arabs will surely have all the more reason to look within to find the ways towards modernity rather than, as previously, seek them in a more or less constrained dialogue with the West. And then, in the confusion which the future could bring, is it not the religious well-springs of political life which will prevail?

'The Mediterranean idea'

Some rare periods of history have seen exchange and dialogue prevail over rivalry and confrontation in the Mediterranean and encouraged some generous-spirited intellectuals on both shores to attempt to give substance to a common Mediterranean ideology. It drew sustenance from memories of Andalusia, where Islam, Judaism, and Christianity had produced a meeting-place of civilizations and cultural creativity of a richness rarely seen again. But this exceptional and special moment in history was a brief one. Except during the far-off days of the Roman empire, the reality of the Mediterranean has always, from the Crusades to the colonization of modern times, been made with conflict and blood. Nevertheless, confrontation can also give rise to exchanges and mutual enrichment.

The Mediterranean idea was based on an intuition that all links forged in mutual distrust or resulting from historical conflicts could be reassessed in a positive light as the foundation for a new adventure of civilization, to be embarked upon

together. However, this thought process was not free from
ambiguities, which did not dampen enthusiasm in some cultural
circles in Europe, particularly France, but did diminish support
on the Arab side. Even in the Maghreb countries, where long-
standing familiarity and many shared illusions have always
facilitated common passions, there were evident hesitations; in
many of those colloquia of the kind where academics usually
work through new and uncertain ideas, speakers from the
Maghreb would usually balance a positive approach to the
'Mediterranean concept' with a parallel and heavily stressed
reference to their own Arab-Islamic identity. In other words, the
attractions of the Mediterranean ideology would rapidly come
to an end if the commitment to the Mediterranean obliged them
to give up a part of their heritage.

Beyond the internal coherence of this cautious approach, other
more political elements were strengthening Arab doubts about
the Europeans' Mediterranean discourse. Europe's global policy
on the region and the overall organization of cooperation, which
the Europeans claimed they wanted to set up as early as possible,
were seen as a cover for political manoevres (notably the insertion
of Israel into the region) and a potential source of further
divisions in the Arab community through the use of over-
simplified criteria to determine operational units on a geographical basis. Moreover, by exploiting the common construction of the Mediterranean project as a set of ideas without
any real substance, the Europeans could be accused of attempting
to put off the full costs which a real solidarity would have
incurred and which would have gone a long way towards
remedying the economic and social inequalities between the two
shores.

Generally speaking, these suspicions regarding the Mediterranean project, which existed at different levels and in different
spheres, can only have grown stronger as a result of the Gulf
war. The invasion of Kuwait was unanimously condemned in
the Arab world, but the chance patiently to explore ways of
finding an Arab solution to the crisis was rejected in favour of a
logic of conflict; the European Community and its two member

states represented on the UN Security Council aligned themselves to all intents and purposes with the American position. In this context, what confidence can the Arabs have in the Mediterranean approach of a Community which, ignoring or under-estimating the effects of its choices on Arab societies, validates and accentuates their divisions?

Granted, the inevitable North–South collaboration which is implied in the nature of things in the Mediterranean cannot be rejected (for the protection of the environment, the coordination of agricultural trade or the regulation of migratory flows, for instance). But if the Mediterranean idea, in its present, creative stage of woolliness, is to become (again) an idea with a promise of the future, if it is not to fall irredeemably into discredit, the minimal conditions for confidence must be restored. To do this, it will be necessary to go beyond the Mediterranean region (unless the Mediterranean stretches as far as Basra, Masqat, Aden, and Khartoum!). The most pressing need is to re-establish a dialogue between Europe and the Arab world as a whole. But obviously it must not be reduced to the institutionalized 'Euro-Arab Dialogue' dating from the mid-1970s, which even the French-inspired relaunch at the end of 1989 did not succeed in transforming into an effective, operational forum for discussion. This dialogue, whilst taking into account the direct reality of Arab states and governments whose positions will be even more divergent if anything after the present crisis, should also, if not primarily, be aimed at the Arab peoples whose experiences of frustration and injustice today will shape the choices of tomorrow.

In other words, the fresh wounds of the Arab peoples will only heal over if rapid changes in Community Europe cause it to review its relationship with the Arab world with a real will and the determination not to act simply as back-up and financier for a regional policy worked out in Washington, and taking full prior account of the stakes, and if it is led to use its full influence in the major problems of the region. These are also the conditions which would allow the construction of a Europe-Mediterranean project to leave behind its present image of an uncertain sub-set and finally to gain acceptance as a viable sphere of cooperation and sharing.

The main problems which need to be tackled in order for EC Europe's credibility to be restored are well known. They are namely: immediate justice for the Palestinians, full and effective implementation of the Taef agreements made in Taef in Saudi Arabia and confirmation of Lebanon's territorial integrity, a dramatic reduction in inequalities of development, arms control, and the security of the whole region (and it should be added that the region's security must not depend on an outside policeman, and should be worked out in a way which pays equal attention to Arab fears and Israeli concerns). To say that the beginnings of a real will to action in Europe are only faintly perceptible is to put it mildly. However, there is no doubt that this is the direction in which the EC could and should work, if it wants to help to wipe the slate clean of the misunderstandings and deep resentments which its lack of boldness and the distortion of its intentions have aroused in the Arab countries.

The France–Maghreb relationship

The least one can say is that French public opinion, which in the main rallied to what was presented to it as the sole standard of Law, did not understand the mobilization of public opinion in the Maghreb countries or the spread of anti-French feeling. It was therefore at a loss to explain why in Rabat, Algiers, and Tangiers it was the intellectuals most open to change, most committed to the process of strengthening of democracy and least suspected of sympathy or indulgence towards the Iraqi regime who were also the strongest critics of France's position.

The reasons can be analysed in detail, but one in particular deserves special attention because it will determine the conditions for any future renewal of dialogue. The disappointment of the Maghreb countries was equal to the hopes raised by François Mitterrand (despite his initial hesitations and the regret expressed at inadequate support for the search for an Arab solution) in his speech before the United Nations on 25 September 1990. When, with France's backing, the logic of ultimatum prevailed over the logic of embargo, then when the shelling of Iraq began, the crack became a split and the split became an open wound. But again, the question arises of how to explain the violence of the reactions, which even the independence struggles, particularly the Algerian war, did not arouse. The reason here is perhaps that those struggles were fought in the name of values— emancipation and the restoration of national identity, social revolution—which were in tune with, indeed directly inspired by, the values proclaimed and often upheld by the colonizing people.

In some ways, the old conflicts took place within a framework of familiar references and all the solidarities between political activists which it allowed. This did not take anything away from the brutality of the conflicts; everyone knows that hatreds and fights within a family are among the most bloody; but the family stays in place. Whatever the regime and its doctrinal inspiration, neither newly-acquired independence, political and institutional breaks nor the vain search for economic independence ever ended in a real split from the old colonizer. This is illustrated, among other things, by the lasting vitality in the Maghreb of the concept of co-development which, in response to the changes required by the economic liberalism which had emerged triumphant on the world scale, called on France to tame and control the blind forces of the economy politically within an organized space—a 'family' space, as it were.

The French position in the Gulf war appeared suddenly to show the illusions and the limits of this relationship. By seeming unconcerned to preserve the links which normally it sought to uphold, by turning a blind eye to the emotion of the Arab popular response to the Iraqi people's suffering, and by agreeing to back to the hilt an undertaking with rather dubious motives, France in a way broke the close link which had united it through thick and thin with the Maghreb countries. Anxious to protect its state interests in the short term (to safeguard its permanent seat on the Security Council and to save the construction of European integration from too strong pressures), France abandoned the more ambitious steps which would have been possible and would have taken account of Arab expectations. With that decision, France found itself reduced to its real status, that of a middle-ranking power; in the Maghreb countries, France's choice caused a psychological break on a scale which should not be under-estimated. In a way, a liberation of minds, a mental decolonization has taken place; the mental break which had been avoided for so long finally took place. From now on, France's partners in the Maghreb will be more autonomous, less friendly, more demanding interlocutors. In some respects, the relationship will finally be made healthier, freed from the condescension, unconscious mimicry and complacency which were not entirely absent before. It is perhaps a good thing. Like the European–Arab dialogue and the Mediterranean idea, the relationship between France and the Maghreb countries can only become again a real project for the future if it proceeds from the reality of facts and equal will on all sides.

The New International Order

*Gianni de Michelis**

CONTEMPORARY EUROPEAN AFFAIRS: *Minister, for several years, and especially since your involvement with the foreign policy of the European Community, you have drawn people's attention to the security problems of the countries in the Mediterranean region. The Gulf War seems to have confirmed your worries and has posed in a very dramatic way the problem of relations between Europe and its Mediterranean environment. How do you interpret the origin and the nature of the conflict?*

GIANNI DE MICHELIS: Naturally, the main reason for the Gulf War was the ambitions and will to power of Saddam Hussein. He created an enormous war machine capable of creating enormous upheaval in the Middle East and threatening a range of countries further afield. In a certain way, the war broke this extremely dangerous spiral, thanks to the firmness of the international community and the unity within the coalition, which enabled the UN resolutions to be upheld..

Having said that, the roots of the war lie also in the precarity of the Middle East region itself, a situation which offered Saddam Hussein, and other false prophets of Islam, the opportunity to hide their true ambitions. As far as I am concerned, before the occupation of Kuwait, I had already raised on several occasions the problem of the instability of the Mediterranean and Gulf regions. I did this very explicitly, on one occasion among many,

* Italian Foreign Minister.

in Paris in December 1988 at a meeting of European Community and Arab Foreign Ministers.

I have on many occasions pointed out the precariousness of the situation; the economic disparities and the demographic pressures, and the complex interrelationships in the zone stretching from Morocco to Iran. The Gulf War has made even more obvious the clear instability in this area. We have seen how the events in Iraq have had immediate repercussions in the Western Mediterranean area. In the absence of a wider system of guarantees, defence structures, such as the Gulf Cooperation Council, have proved themselves inadequate to contain the Iraqi threat. Our view on the Middle East is based upon our recognition of a whole range of instabilities and inadequacies. And this should be borne in mind in the aftermath of the war if we wish to build a lasting peace.

CEA: *Do you think, Minister, that the break that the war has occasioned will have serious consequences on North–South relations, and do you think that the Arab countries will become more radical, a development which will make dialogue even more difficult?*

GDM: Saddam Hussein's defeat should be seen by the Arab world as the thousandth humiliation, as the negation of the historical aspirations that the Iraqi despot claimed to represent. We saw it in the demonstrations of solidarity with Iraq by some of the Mediterranean countries, and in Jordan where there is a strong Palestinian presence.

This feeling springs in part from unsolved problems, in particular, the Arab–Israeli conflict. Throughout the crisis, the Community tried to ensure that Saddam Hussein was not identified with the Arab cause, and that the Western coalition was not seen as another crusade.

Since the beginning of August, during Italy's presidency of the Council, we strove to ensure that international law be observed strictly under the aegis of the United Nations. Saddam Hussein's defeat should not be treated as a show of force by the United States but as a demonstration of the authority of the UN.

Moreover, throughout this period, we have stressed on many occasions the need to think seriously and constructively about the future equilibrium of the Middle East, in order that we manage the peace properly. This approach places the action of the coalition in the wider perspective of the introduction of new rules for the future coexistence between states.

That is the positive way we have worked in order that the war does not create an unbridgeable gap between the Arab world and Europe, between the West and Islam.

CEA: *You were one of those who started the Conferences on Security and Cooperation in the Mediterranean which has linked the question of security to that of development in the Mediterranean area. How, in reality, can this relationship be operated?*

GDM: There has been a general movement towards bringing together security and development as if they were two sides of the same coin. We see it in Europe where the issue of aggression from Eastern Europe has diminished. However, the uncertainties linked to economic changes in Eastern Europe bring new and unknown problems with them.

In the Middle East, the rhythm of changes, the rampant unemployment, and the demographic pressures are all factors contributing to the instability which could reduce, even paralyse, the ability of the political class to govern. Such a situation encourages all kinds of radical solutions and of course fundamentalism, and it creates real opportunities to the hegemonic ambitions of adventurers such as Saddam Hussein. It also puts pressure on the Mediterranean borders of the Community, where there is continuous border traffic. Our security will also depend upon the degree of poverty that we are prepared to tolerate outside the privileged boundaries of the European Community.

Hence the idea of a Conference on Security and Cooperation in the Mediterranean and Middle East, in order to see a wider perspective that is extended geographically to all of the problems in the region. Taking as its model the Helsinki accords, this conference should codify a series of rules and principles related to security, economic cooperation, and respect for fundamental freedoms.

CEA: *In the present context, can Europe have a specific role to play? How do you interpret the fact that in the crisis itself Europe was unable to express itself with a single voice? Does this mean that the road to unity has, in fact, hardly begun?*

GDM: The Community was univocal throughout the period of sanctions. It reacted rapidly, and just two days after the invasion of Kuwait, it adopted restrictive measures in its economic relations with Iraq, a situation which encouraged other international bodies to act in a similar way.

The Community was also active in its attempts to respond to the consequences of the crisis. It contributed to maintaining cohesion as regards sanctions, by helping certain countries affected by the embargo because it hoped that if the sanctions were maintained, then military force would prove unnecessary.

On the other hand, Europe did prove to be quite inadequate, in relation to its ambitions and resources, once the conflict began. In spite of the potential coordination that the Western European Union offered, it was soon clear how limited the scope of the Community was to undertake a coordinated recourse to arms. From this we concluded that what was needed was to accelerate political union and to ensure, at the foreign policy and security level, a common defence within the wider framework of the Atlantic Alliance.

CEA: *Much has been said about a new role for the United Nations. Do you think that the war has strengthened this view or not? What is your response to the UN Secretary General, Mr Perez de Cuellar's claim that this was not the UN's war? Do you think it is necessary to change the composition of the Security Council, democratize its internal workings? What do you think of the German's attitude and their request for a united Germany to participate in the Security Council?*

GDM: Perez de Cuellar has said that this war was not the UN's war in the sense that the coalition's troops were not under the UN flag. But it was overall a UN action because the international coalition was fighting in order to get Saddam Hussein to accept the twelve resolutions adopted by the Security Council after the invasion of Kuwait. What is at stake in the Gulf is precisely the ability of the UN, not only to draw up the rules, but also to have them respected. For the first time since its creation, we have avoided the entanglements and dead-ends of the vetos of the permanent members, who in the past paralysed its workings.

The change in Eastern Europe had already opened up the possibility of a new set of international relations, based upon dialogue, respect for basic rights, instead of the oldest law of the abuse of power. Ensuring that Saddam Hussein did not prevail means that thanks to the language and institutions of the UN this process might be extended to the whole world. Besides, this was a UN war also in the sense that the UN's rules should help us to better construct a future peace, and not only in the recent combat zone.

It is also true that the institutions of the United Nations reflect a past reality, that of the immediate post-war period. That is why I have been a long time supporter, especially since the reunification of Germany and the end of the cold war, of the idea that we should now re-examine certain aspects of the UN; and especially if we wish to make the UN a microcosm of a future world government. It is not enough to integrate a united Germany into the Security Council as a permanent member. We need to rethink the composition of the Security Council, increase the number of its permanent members to include, among others, Germany, Japan, and Italy. We also need to reflect upon the possibility of distributing the vote within the Security Council which would reflect the varying weight and influence of each of its members.

CEA: *People also speak of a new international order. How do you see this? What should be the role of the USSR in this new order?*

GDM: The new international order has grown out of a respect

for the principles expressed within different institutions from the UN to the Arab League and the Conference on Security and Cooperation in Europe. These principles involve respect for the sovereignty of states, the non-use of force, the inviolability of fundamental rights, respect for human dignity, and minimal acceptable standards of living and economic development.

We believe that everyone should work to contribute to this new order. In the Middle East, I believe that a strong consensus will emerge from the countries in the area on the question of security, a security that will have strong local roots but which will also enjoy international support. We are counting on the Soviet Union to help shape this new world. Its contribution will be a decisive one in the changes taking place on the European continent, and this is in part thanks to a Soviet foreign policy which has placed the well-being and security of the USSR in a completely new framework, namely collaboration and integration at the continental level.

The Soviet Union, therefore, could help bring us closer to world government which, even in this century, after two world wars, were the aspirations of both Presidents Wilson and Roosevelt, among others. In the Gulf Crisis, the Soviet contribution has been in accordance with this view. That is the reason why we have appreciated Gorbachev's efforts to obtain a withdrawal from Kuwait before the beginning of the ground offensive, efforts that were frustrated by the obstinacy of Saddam Hussein. One important aspect of the Soviet commitment will be its participation, alongside the most advanced Western countries, in a collective effort to cope with the problem of arms sales to Third World countries.

CEA: *At the heart of this new world order there is the problem of the distribution of wealth, especially for the countries of the South and the Mediterranean area, especially as regards a fairer management of oil resources and revenue; and for the North there remains the question of access to energy supplies. How do you see these issues?*

GDM: At the heart of a different international order there are problems of development and instability which have no precedent, both at the demographic level and at the environmental level. In the Middle East, it will be essential to find a more equal distribution of wealth, not only amongst the countries in the area but also in terms of the European countries, the United States and Japan. A more sensible use of energy resources is one of the keys to a new future. And recently, there has been much discussion on the question of the proper management in the Middle East of the water supply. Whatever happens, I think myself that the southern hemisphere should benefit from a new solidarity, both in quantitative and qualitative terms.

The Italian Presidency of the Council put forward as early as July 1990 the proposal that 1% of the GDP of the Twelve be given in aid to Eastern Europe, the Mediterranean area, and the Third World, ·25% for each of the first two categories and ·5% for the third.

Even at that time we suggested the setting up of a financial institution which would deal with the Mediterranean area, along the lines of the European Bank for the reconstruction and development of the Eastern European countries.

Our ideas have been part of a more general rethinking and reflection being undertaken by the Twelve. And we saw many of these ideas reemerge in the Commission document on the role of the Community in the Mediterranean after the end of the Gulf crisis. The need for a specific financial institution for this area has also been stressed by the American Secretary of State, James Baker, during a congressional debate on the future of the Middle East. This demonstrates that ideas, when they are good ones, take on a strength and life of their own.

Lessons for After the War

*Pierre Mauroy**

CONTEMPORARY EUROPEAN AFFAIRS: *First Secretary, now that the war is over and Iraq has accepted the United Nations resolutions, what lessons do you draw from this war?*

PIERRE MAUROY: The first thing to say is that it is by no means clear that the ceasefire on 28 February means that we have peace. Nevertheless, several lessons can already be drawn from the Gulf War.

The first is related to the overall system of international relations. The context of the two superpowers confronting each other in a military stalemate has come to an end afer 45 years. Saddam Hussein did not choose the best moment to annex Kuwait. For years, the UN was paralysed because of the East–West divide. Today, it has asserted its authority, and allowed international law to regain its meaning and its strength. The collapse of the Soviet Union and the democratization of Eastern Europe have given the international community the opportunity to make its voice heard and condemn the clear violation of the law governing states. The condemnation of Saddam Hussein took place in all countries. The UN decisions were applied and followed by action. The organization that we, as socialists, have striven to see constructed for more than a century, can tomorrow play a major role in the construction of a new international order.

*First Secretary of the French Socialist Party and former Prime Minister.

In this sense, a new chapter is beginning and, one day, history will say that we have already begun the 21st Century. It is true that calling the Gulf War a war about law can seem a tautology because all wars are about legality for those involved in them. On the other hand, I would go so far as to say that this war was legitimized by an international law that was drawn up and voted upon by a truly international organization. Moreover, the texts that were passed have been upheld, and the UN resolutions apply to everyone. In this sense the second lesson will doubtless be that the liberation of Kuwait will be a precedent in international jurisprudence.

The other lessons to be drawn from the Gulf War will be shaped by the way the peace itself is handled. We must move as quickly as possible from the ceasefire to the peace. Kuwait has been freed, in accordance with the UN mandate. The disappearance of thousands of men and women, the scale of destruction, and the ecological catastrophe are illustrations of the cruelty of the months of occupation. And if evidence were needed, they emphasize a posteriori the legitimacy of the coalition's action. Sticking only to the sanctions of August 1990, would have left Kuwait with no chance to find once again its own identity. The effects of its annexation would have been irreversible.

The new peace must be that of peoples, of their self determination and of democracy. We must therefore avoid any double standards. International law must now be applied in Lebanon and in Palestine, and especially in the area of the Middle East where conflict has been going on for so long and has brought such suffering to the people involved.

CEA: *Has this war not destabilized the regional balance, especially by creating the conditions for a strengthening of the positions of Turkey and Iran? Moreover, do you not think that the defeat of Arab nationalism in its Iraqi form will lead to an upsurge in Islamic fundamentalism, especially in the Shi'ite regions? Also on this question of regional instability, do you not think that this war will weaken the monarchies in the region?*

PM: What brought the war about was the regional disequilibrium in favour of Iraq. It is true that the Middle East can only be stabilized if the countries involved, Iraq, Syria, Iran, Saudi Arabia, but also Egypt and Turkey, find some kind of economic, demographic, military, and political equilibrium. Iraq believed after its bloody eight-year war with Iran that it could solve its historical border disputes and gain access to the sea via Kuwait. Saudi Arabia decided to appeal for the military assistance of its allies in the face of its powerful neighbour. Syria, for its part, saw in the affair a way of weakening its traditional enemy, Iraq. So we have to recognize that the seeds of destabilization were there before the military intervention, and that all the initiatives in the region designed to resolve the dispute had failed. To answer your question fully, I would add that after the war, nothing will be like it was before, neither in the Middle East nor in the international arena. The democratic imperative is making itself felt in Eastern Europe, in Latin America, in the Maghreb, as well as in the Middle East. For us, this right is indivisible, and is not negotiable either. Whether faced with dictatorship or monarchies, democrats demand respect for human rights, and respect for democracy. The Gulf War has brought these issues closer, but it is true that time is needed, and a lot of patience. All steps in this direction should, however, be given our support. You do not further the rights of people by allowing a dictator to violate those rights and get away with it. On the contrary.

CEA: *You yourself have often stated that the two key issues are the Palestinian question, and the question of democracy in the region. Do you not think that, on the one hand, the time has come for the Palestinians to express themselves, and that on the other, the encouragement of democracy presupposes the reorganization of the distribution of wealth in the region (that is to say the undermining of the ruling monarchies)?*

PM: For several years we have been stressing that the Palestinian people must achieve a homeland and a state. Their undeniable right to self-determination and to the choice of those who represent them must operate within a democratic context. The Palestinian issue brings to the surface so many passions throughout the Arab world that to ignore it would be to make of the peace a simple postponement of a deeper crisis. We now have the opportunity to build a new regional order, a peace based upon justice, that is to say one which refuses double standards, and which will therefore find a solution to the Palestinian problem. We have been given another chance to sort the problem out. How are we to profit from the occasion, given that in the West Bank and the Gaza strip, after three years of *intifada*, curfew, and the breakdown of the economic infra-structure, and now the fears borne of the war, have frustrated and sometimes left despairing whole generations of young people? How do we seize the opportunity given that Israel itself has recently been the victim of serious aggression in a war that it was not even involved in? We know there are difficulties, but we know also that there is only one way forward: dialogue; only one method: negotiation; only one policy: to find a compromise.

I think that in the longer term the realignments in the Middle East must involve the setting up of structures that will distribute oil resources more fairly, and help economic development. The sharing of oil resources, the redistribution of that other local wealth, namely, water, must involve cooperation, especially given the extremely problematic demographic situation. Economic cooperation between these countries must be the product of their own will, and will help reduce the wastage and the losses. It does presuppose, however, political and military cooperation. Everything has to be done, therefore, in stages. And nothing will be possible on the economic or political level if the situation remains hostile and explosive as it has been for so many years.

CEA: *You have been quoted as having made statements concerning the representativeness of the Palestine Liberation Organization. Could you define very clearly what is the official position of the French Socialist Party regarding this issue?*

PM: In my view, and I have held this view for many years, no cause is more noble and just than that of the Palestinian people and their search for a homeland; and on many occasions, I have been in the forefront of their struggle.

Two significant dates will help us here. In 1982, Yasser Arafat, under siege and attack from the Syrian army, was shielded by the French paratroopers at Tripoli in the Lebanon, and escorted safely to Tunis. In 1989, after the Algiers meeting which implicitly recognized Israel's existence, Arafat came to Paris, where he declared that the PLO's founding charter was obsolete. In order to hail these advances on the road to dialogue I visited Arafat's hotel and on behalf of the French Socialist Party greeted him and encouraged him in his undertaking. On the 16 August, 1990 when I was in Tunis representing President Mitterrand I met Arafat again. He told me he was committed to a peaceful end to the Gulf crisis, and his intention was to maintain a balanced position between Kuwait and Iraq. I noted once again his wisdom, and assured the PLO of France's support for an Arab peace plan.

I feel that by abandoning this position and throwing his organization into an inter-Arab conflict, and by taking the side of the person who scorned law and attacked Israel, Yasser Arafat committed a very serious mistake. A mistake which may very well have serious consequences for the Palestinian cause in the eyes of the international community. I made my view known perfectly clearly on behalf of the French Socialist Party, a party that has had good relations with the PLO for a very long time. I feel I can, therefore, speak frankly to our friends, as I have to my Israeli friends when describing as unacceptable the treatment meeted out to the Palestinians in the occupied territories.

CEA: *Some say that this war has reopened the old hostilities of the Mediterranean region. How do you see the development of relations between the two shores of the Mediterranean? Do you think, for example, that with economic aid (either in the form of loans, or in the form of a bank for Sub-Saharan Africa) these age-old cultural hostilities can be overcome? What do you think of the Algerian Foreign Affairs Minister's view that the Maghreb has been forgotten by France throughout this crisis?*

PM: We need to talk about this. And we began to do so as early as 2 August, 1990. I went to Tunis, Algiers, and Rabat myself on the 10 August. Today, it has to be said that wild adventurism is no solution to accumulated frustrations. The Maghreb's future must come from inside itself, and we will always be supportive. The Maghreb must also learn that it must always be on the side of democracy rather than on the side of dictatorship, whether or not this involves a fellow nation. For the Maghreb, as for us, there is no other way towards justice and peace other than via democracy. And France, like Europe, who only recently abandoned its last dictators, some of which were among the worst the world has ever seen, knows this very well.

Today, once again, we need to say to the Maghreb that a solid friendship survives disagreements but cannot survive a lie. Our destinies are intertwined and dialogue between us constant. I know we shall overcome this and go forward from a new understanding.

CEA: *France has been arguing for some time for not only a new political order, but also a new international economic order. We know that the United States as well as the main international organizations, such as the International Monetary Fund and the World Bank, are not particularly sensitive to French arguments. How do you think France can get its ideas across in an international context that is objectively dominated by a US victory?*

PM: Today, the world has a greater need than ever for cooperation and justice. States are now expected to respond positively, for example, to the historic commitment by the Eastern European countries to democratization. And France wishes to be part of this movement for democracy and justice.

It was France which at the Versailles Summit in 1982 raised, for the first time in a meeting of the industrialized countries, the question of lightening the burden of debt of the poorest countries. It was François Mitterrand who raised the point. Since then, the movement has widened and deepened, important progress has been made and many issues are resolved, and at the great festival in Paris to commemorate the bicentenary of the French Revolution in 1989, it was, again, France who called for a North–South conference. There was no immediate response, but today it is becoming clearer and clearer that we must go much further. The different continents of the planet cannot survive if they go on behaving as if they are in different centuries from one another.

The Gulf War was certainly not a North–South conflict. But part of Arab opinion sees it like this. Those huge demonstrations were, whatever else they were, a call for a more cooperative and just world order. We should not let fundamentalism profit from movements of opinion which are not really related to the will to religious domination or sectarian conflict.

Economic cooperation is essential. Ideas have already been put forward such as that of a bank along the lines of the one that has been set up in conjunction with the Eastern European countries. Perhaps it only needs getting existing organizations and structures—the various inter-Arab funds, the European Investment Bank, and others—to work properly together, and reorientate their objectives towards more specific development programmes.

Dialogue must be based upon open and clear relationships. And in particular—because the values of democracy are universal ones—we must pay particular attention to the countries moving in the direction of democracy, respect for human rights and the exercise of freedom.

The North cannot be blind to what is happening in the South, In fact, to a certain degree, the South is already in the North. France, for example, showed during the Gulf War a profound unity which exceeded our expectations. Far from tearing itself apart, the national community deepened its internal dialogue; and in particular the dialogue between Jews and Muslims. This is a considerable change and one which should be appreciated. It has also created new imperatives of its own.

CEA: *It has often been said that Europe was conspicuous by its absence in this crisis. How do you explain this situation?*

PM: It was not Community impotence that was surprising, given that Europe has neither a common foreign policy nor a military force of its own. The surprise is rather due to the fact that in spite of the handicaps, the Twelve did adopt a series of common positions, and were even able to act, for example, in terms of its naval presence to which nine nations of the Western European Union played a significant part given that they were responsible for two-thirds of the sanctions control. From this, even though we do recognize the gaps and the lessons to be learned, we can be certain too of the acceleration of the integration process. It is in that spirit that the French President called for a special European summit in Luxemburg. We must turn our attention to the Europe of after the Gulf War. We must also think of the economic cooperation that will be necessary with organisations in the region, but also of another major contribution to peace, namely, the control of arms sales, of arms themselves and of their non-proliferation.

Israel and the Gulf War

Elie Barnavi*

The war will probably be over by the time this article leaves the printing press. But at the time of its writing the war is still raging, and although the nature of its outcome is no longer in doubt, no one can foresee exactly when it will end. Besides, the extent of disinformation is such that we have little idea of what exactly is happening.

What we do know is that the consequences of the conflict will be dramatic. The future of the world is at stake in the sands of Arabia, left, as it is, disoriented by the end of the era of antagonistic blocs. But the future of the world is not my concern in this article. This is a conflict between two political cultures, two conceptions of man and the state, two ways of regarding the community of nations. I will restrict myself deliberately to a provincial point of view: the Third World War seen from Israel; and how best to use the Gulf War to the advantage of peace.

It is easy to argue that this is not our war. A megalomaniac dictator, a good thousand kilometres from Tel Aviv, has devoured a neighbouring state; the aggressor and the victim speak the same language, practice the same religion and are even members of the same Arab nation—so why should it concern us? After all, it would require a good deal of political myopia, or hate—the two frequently go together—to ignore the obvious: that Saddam Hussein would have invaded Kuwait even if the hated 'Zionist state' had not existed. There were many excellent

* Professor at the University of Tel Aviv.

reasons why and everyone is aware of them. But there is one which nobody mentions but which to me seems primordial: the nature of the Iraqi régime condemns it to expansionism. After eight years of war with a disappointing outcome, and still in possession of an enormous army, the search for a new enemy was the obvious next step. To understand the man and his régime, two books are indispensable: *The Origins of Totalitarianism* by Hannah Arendt, and Sartre's *L'Enfance d'un chef*. What has Israel got to do with all this? Nothing of course.

That remains the case even if the perspective is reversed and we view the conflict from the side of the anti-Iraq coalition. To say that the Americans are pursuing the war against Saddam for the sake of the Zionists (this has, after all, been said) is to subscribe to the same logic as those who once said that the Americans fought Hitler on behalf of the Jewish international. The common front of extreme right, Communists, and pacifists has been reconstituted under the fascinated gaze of historians. In reply to a journalist who asked why he was firing missiles at a non-belligerent country, Saddam, with a smile of pity at such naïveté, replied: 'Because it is Israel'. The Protocol of the Elders of Zion refuses to go away.

Besides, it is obvious that no-one is fighting for Israel in the Gulf—neither the Americans, nor the Europeans, nor the Syrians, Saudis, and Egyptians, an unlikely coalition which is concerned above all to keep Israel out of the conflict. They are fighting for a host of reasons, good and bad, among which figure, to varying degrees depending on the country, the fear of a dictator with a fierce appetite for power, economic interests, a desire to put an end to practices which are incompatible with the rules of international behaviour, and the need to build a new world order on the debris of the now defunct bipolar Cold War system; and also, of course, to avoid giving any satisfaction or sense of legal or moral triumph to the champions of a false *realpolitik* which is entirely based on enmity towards the United States.

* * *

But in reality this war is also well and truly ours. First of all *physically*, because the Iraqi dictator has done all he can to bring us into it, because the sirens have been wailing from Dao to Beer-Sheba, and because for five weeks, a people who have not fired one shot, have been carrying or wearing gasmasks, and have been living in terror of the Scuds. Of course, no-one here gave much credibility to Saddam's blustering or believed that he would really be able to 'burn half of Israel'; and from the purely military point of view, operation 'Desert Shield' has been a godsend for the Israelis. The destruction of Iraq's military potential is certain, as is perhaps the elimination of Saddam's régime; thus while Israel has contributed nothing towards the prosecution of the war, this will not prevent it from being one of its main beneficiaries. For the Jewish state, in effect, the alternative could be posed in very simple terms: the Americans today; or us tomorrow. This expansionist adversary, who has made no secret of his desire to assume the leadership of the Arab world in the name of hatred for Israel, had an army of one and a half million soldiers and a formidable arsenal of conventional, chemical, and biological weapons, as well as a potential nuclear capacity. All the better for Israel if an international coalition under the umbrella of the UN destroys the 'western front' of this power. All the same, before that could occur, Saddam succeeded in imposing on the Israelis what we call here 'the routine of a state of emergency'.

Second, *psychologically*, this has been a novel but extremely distressing experience for Israel. Half a century of uninterrupted war in extremely difficult conditions—including territorial constraints, the hostility of neighbouring peoples, continuous attempts to question and undermine the legitimacy of Israel's existence, and perpetual isolation on the international scene— has created a collective siege mentality.

This, in turn, has helped produce a military doctrine based on three simple principles: never leave aggression unpunished, prevent it as often as possible, and hit back quickly and forcefully to deter any repetition. Israel is the puny, highly strung schoolboy who must constantly prove himself to the big boys. Now all of that has been thrown into question by Iraq's strategy of terror. Israel has been forced to walk on its head; the rear has become the front, women and old people have found themselves on the front line, and the civil defence force, traditionally treated with condescension, is the only one to have been mobilized. An unreal battle, with victims but no soldiers, in which all of the military and civil norms of the country have been overturned. It is obviously too early to assess the impact of all this on the psychology of the Israelis. But even if we are not yet in a position to gauge the consequences, it is already obvious that they will be considerable.

Finally, the war is also ours for *political* reasons. To understand why requires a more detailed analysis.

* * *

In the first place it seems clear that the war will do nothing to alter the political divide within Israel itself. As always, each of the two camps has found confirmation of its own long-held views in the event of the Gulf war. For the right, Iraqi provocation has proved that the essence of the Arab–Israeli Conflict remains the inter-state struggle, the alignment of the PLO 'proving' once again the intrinsic perversity of the Palestinian organization. For the left, the Scuds have shown how illusory is the country's security which the occupied territories supposedly provide. Momentarily disarmed by the policies of Arafat and by the enthusiasm of the Palestinian masses for the new Saladin, the proponents of peace quickly regained their composure; the hub of the problem for them remains the same—seeking a historic compromise with the Palestinian people. Between these two positions, public opinion has been disorientated and anxious, and expects simply that the government fulfils its task and governs effectively, and that the political class as a whole does its job—i.e., defining clear political options so that the people can make their own choice in the knowledge that they have been properly informed.

On the other side of the barricades, the situation is much

worse. Blinded by hate, the Palestinian masses have given themselves body and soul to a man and a policy which have been disastrous for their cause; as for their leaders, they have simply done Mossad (the Israeli secret service) an enormous favour. To have backed with such consistency a bad horse, to have followed the passions of the crowd instead of channelling them, to have discredited everywhere the cause that they were supposed to serve—Mr Arafat and his friends truly deserve to be confronted by the Likud.

Clearly no solution will emerge from the two societies embroiled in a conflict which they are incapable of resolving themselves; it will be imposed from outside, principally by the United States which wants to use the Gulf crisis to find a final solution to the problems of the Middle East.

*　　*　　*

The Gulf war has revealed the truth of a situation whose consequences will remain with us for some time to come: ironically, Israel, like Iraq, is the victim of the collapse of the bipolar world order and the new-found strength of the United States. In the bipolar system of the Cold War, Israel, a solid member of the western camp, provided a legitimate strategic link for the United States in a region which was vital to the interests of both super powers; this is no longer the case. Whether in bringing the men of Baghdad to justice, ensuring the stability of the region, guaranteeing the flow of oil in conditions of reasonable security and at reasonable prices, reducing the terrorist menace, or in backing régimes which are open to Western interests, Riyad, Cairo, Teheran, or even Damascus are much more useful to the Americans than Jerusalem. Thus, for the Israeli right, the coalition put together by the US administration has been a catastrophe.

Thus, also, it is obvious why despite the prudent overtures periodically made by the Americans towards Israel (which have aimed primarily to prevent it from spoiling the coalition party) relations between the United States and Israel have never been so equivocal. Even during the course of the war—between two enthusiastic speeches about the 'remarkable restraint' shown by Jerusalem—the Americans refused to provide a governmental guarantee for a loan of 400 million dollars to be used for integrating Soviet immigrants into Israeli society. This was because they had not been satisfied by Israeli assurances concerning construction in the occupied territories; and rather moderate criticisms from the Israeli ambassador to Washington (once again concerning the 400 million dollars which had been promised many times but indefinitely postponed) provoked a reaction from the White House like a slap in the face; the Secretary of State James Baker used the occasion to announce the broad outlines of a new post-war regional order which were guaranteed to make the Shamir cabinet break into a cold sweat. One could draw up a list of similar 'misunderstandings'—a modest euphemism—to illustrate this point. The clearest thinkers on the Israeli right have long understood—and they are now beginning to state it publicly—that not only do the interests of the Americans not coincide with those of Israel (at least in the way they are defined by the right-wing coalition in power in Jerusalem) but that they are completely at odds.

*   *   *

The key word of course is *linkage*, the famous connection that Saddam has sought to make between the crisis in the Gulf and the Arab–Israeli conflict. The idea of linkage is both ill-founded and useful. Why is this so? It is ill-founded because the occupation of Kuwait by Iraq does not have a lot to do with the occupation of the West Bank, the Golan Heights, and the Gaza Strip by Israel, and the community of nations has rightly rejected this spurious comparison. First of all, the Golan Heights excepted, the territories conquered by Israel in June 1967 were under the control of countries whose sovereignty there was either universally contested, by the Arab states themselves (the West Bank) or was exerted temporarily over a population which was deprived of its citizenship (Gaza). Iraq, by contrast, took possession of a sovereign state which was recognized as such by the community of nations. Also, concerned at the danger of isolation in the international arena and fearful of alienating an important segment of public opinion—public opinion does actually count in Israel—successive governments in Jerusalem have refrained from formally annexing these territories. Kuwait, on the other hand, has been devastated, depopulated, terrorized and transformed into an Iraqi province. Finally, and most importantly, the territories conquered by Israel were taken over following a defensive war, conducted against enemies who had explicitly called for its destruction; I was not aware of any similar threat posed to Iraq by *its* neighbour. Also the two issues should be carefully separated. Otherwise, Saddam Hussein will receive a sort of 'reward for aggression' which will allow him to save face while in no way providing a solution to the problem of Israeli occupation of Arab territory.

But at the same time the concept of *linkage* is useful, on condition that we know how to use it well. Even after the Iraqi aggression has been repulsed, the link between the two issues will inevitably re-emerge. Because no matter how different the two situations, I cannot see how the community of nations will accept a state of affairs in Israel that it has refused to countenance in Kuwait. Also it is improbable that the West in general, and the United States in particular, would take the risk of being accused, with good justification, of impartiality in this respect by its erstwhile Arab allies (members of a coalition which was mounted after all, against one of their brother states); or that they would light-heartedly allow this embryonic international order (the rationale, after all for creating the coalition) to fall so quickly into ruin. A good way of avoiding this would be to get Jerusalem to pay the debt contracted by Washington in Damascus, Cairo, and Riyad. This does in fact appear to be Washington's intention.

Thus, for the partisans of peace in both camps, present circumstances would appear to be propitious. It would be tragic to allow the extremists to spoil them.

The Financial Consequences of the Gulf War

Pierre Bérégovoy*

CONTEMPORARY EUROPEAN AFFAIRS:*Could you tell us straight away, Minister, what you think will be the economic consequences for France of the Gulf War, and for European integration more generally?*

PIERRE BÉRÉGOVOY: It is still too early to make an economic analysis of the Gulf War. Iraq has pulled out of Kuwait, but the political climate which pervades the Iraqi dictator's defeat is still difficult to perceive very well. I think that this confrontation will have produced the beginning of a new international economic order, an order that has been long overdue. The Gulf War was inevitable given the behaviour of Saddam Hussein and his desire to dominate that part of the world. But it is true also that Hussein's pretexts were provided for him. Too much wealth coexists with too much poverty, and we should profit from the new political circumstances to redistribute the oil more fairly, and organize a more balanced development in the region. The great powers, the members of the Security Council in particular, have a fundamental responsibility to help alleviate this. There are immediate economic consequences of the war: a fall in the price of oil and the rebuilding of Kuwait and Iraq will create great potential for economic growth. The lower price of oil will create greater spending power in the industrialized countries and will help them avoid inflation. The rebuilding of Kuwait and Iraq will require capital and, of course, will provide work in the

* French Minister of Finance.

Middle East. Having said this, this does not mean that the war in itself has solved the planet's economic problems. Investment needs are significant in the industrialized countries; and are even more necessary in Eastern Europe. Everything has to be rethought as regards the Third World whose debt crisis is severe. Perhaps we should profit from the current circumstances to look again at these problems from the global perspective.

The United Nations' new-found authority can, of course, help France's own particular concern for help and assistance to be given to the developing countries.

CEA: *On the question of collective effort, for some weeks now there has been a debate in France over the question of the costs of the war. Some people have asked whether the war has been used as a pretext to increase the austerity measures, even though the slowing down of the economy does not justify such measures. Does the financing of the war involve cuts in public spending, or will it involve a special tax? What is your view?*

PB: I see no confusion in government policy on this issue, namely the cost of the war, about 12 billion francs out of a budget of 1300 billion. Let me stress that the Gulf War is not a pretext for anything, but a reality which complicates the economic situation both because of the costs of the military effort, and because of the need for solidarity with the front-line states such as Turkey, Egypt, and Jordan. We have already taken into account the slowing down of the world economy. On top of the costs of the Gulf War we have to add our contribution to Europe and the new minimum wage. The whole thing comes to about 12 billion francs. The decision to pay for this 12 billion francs by savings elsewhere has been given support right across the political spectrum.

CEA: *This is over and above the 20 billion already cut from the 1991 budget?*

PB: No, it is over and above nothing. We had a decision to take, and, like all decisions, it was a difficult one. The first possibility was to let the budgetary deficit grow, which would have put off the lowering of interest rates, or indeed caused them to rise, which would have been a further expense for French producers. The interest rates cost French business something like 24 billion francs. The second possibility was to increase taxes. At a time when internal demand was falling—there has been, in fact, a fall in consumer spending, and we are preparing ourselves for a similar fall in investment—an extra tax is not a welcome thing. For both economic and perhaps also psychological reasons we felt it was better to avoid the taxation option. The third possibility, and this is what I did, along with the Prime Minister, Michel Rocard, was to go for spending cuts. The question raised, however, is whether we shall be faced with more spending in the coming months. The issue will involve the same questions, the same sacrifices; and we must do all we can to avoid an interest rate rise and a further slowing down of economic activity. There will be many points of view expressed, and I shall give my own view when the time comes. But if governing is about foresight, it does not necessarily mean that it should plan for the most pessimistic scenario possible, and the 20 billion francs you were talking about. The budget was passed with a public spending figure which will rise 4.8% from 1990 to 1991. Public spending is not going down. It can tolerate an extra 12 or 20 billion franc demand upon it; I prefer the lower figure.

CEA: *Let us turn, Minister, to the question of Europe, before going on to discuss North–South relations. One can ask today whether through this Gulf crisis there has not been a kind of division of labour between France and Germany; Germany the banker, and France, if not the military authority in Europe, then the country most influential in setting Europe's political orientation?*

PB: France condemned the invasion of Kuwait, and its annexation. France is a member of the United Nations, as is Germany. It is also a permanent member of the Security Council. It therefore decided not simply to condemn the invasion on paper but to be actively involved in the Security Council's decisions and their application. France played its part in accordance with its commitments to the international community. The United Nations Charter applies to everyone. Some countries recognized this, for others, sometimes because of their constitutions, as is the case of Germany and of Japan, it was more difficult. I will not say anything more on that: France fulfills its responsibilities as a permanent member of the Security Council and as a signatory of the UN Charter. It would be highly desirable to create a basis for agreement at the European level, where each one of us contributes according to our role in the conflict. France will be heavily involved in the many international conferences which will grow out of the current situation in an effort to solve the problems created by it. I hope France will be, alongside Great Britain, and others including Germany, the spokesperson not only for the interests of Europe, but also for the will of Europe to organize in a peaceful way the countries of the region.

CEA: *The United States is in recession, and has said that its economy was in a very difficult situation. It has accepted reducing its interest rates. Germany, on the other hand, has refused to reduce its interest rates. What will be the effects of all this on the French economy?*

PB: We have here, in fact, a disagreement between the Federal Reserve Bank and the Bundesbank. The former reduced its rates, the latter put them up. France has not changed its interest rates at all. Of course, the interest rates here in France are linked to those at the global level and to the rates inside the European Monetary System. But our economy's good health has allowed us not to follow the Bundesbank in raising our rates. The interest rates in the money markets in France have been going down.

France is in a good economic position. Inflation is under control, the budgetary deficit has been held in acceptable limits. Did you know that Federal Germany will have a public deficit of 4% less than GDP in 1991; in France it will be 1.2%. This means that there are problems in the German money market, and the Bundesbank has clearly wanted to send out a warning to the federal government that it should reduce the deficit. Even if we work together inside the EMS, interest rates will not be the same in each country. At the beginning of 1988 the French and German interest rates were 4 to 5% apart. Today, the rate differs between 0.5 and 0.75 of a percentage point. This means that France has, thanks to its having sorted out its economy, a significant margin for manoeuvre; and all this, of course, within the framework of European economic and monetary cooperation. We shall exploit this margin at the appropriate moment.

It is true that I would have preferred the Germans and the Americans to have done the same in accordance with the G7 communiqué of January 1991, that is to say, the communiqué concerning the lowering of the rate. We must avoid the twin risks of inflation and recession. It is clear that Germany thinks more about inflation, American more about recession. Taking into account the reduction in the price of oil by about 20 dollars a barrel, it seems obvious to me that the danger of inflation has receded and that we should now do everything to ensure that activity gets underway again.

CEA: *Do you not think that this reduction in the price of oil is only temporary?*

PB: That is possible. In September 1990 in Washington I spoke in favour of an appropriate price for oil. I have never thought that it would rise to 40 dollars, because there is an abundant supply. There is always a disequilibrium if there is strong supply and a reduced demand. The price of oil is thus forced down. But sudden fluctuations should be avoided. 40 dollars a barrel is too high, if tomorrow it falls to 12 dollars, that would be too low for the producing countries who have enormous costs to cover. It would be good if the international community could organize the oil market in a balanced way. I have often said that oil is not a raw material like the others; sometimes it is the consumer who is adversely affected, sometimes it is the producers. We need to regulate the oil market. France has made a con-tribution to this by commissioning a report on the subject. I have made some suggestions myself; I think, in particular, that we must think about a possible reorganization of the market of oil products. It will be difficult. We made efforts to organize the currency market, and with some success since 1985, because we felt that money is not a commodity like others. It should be the same for oil in the present world economic conjuncture; oil is not a raw material like others, as indeed has been demonstrated by the oil producing countries organising themselves into OPEC since 1973. It is extremely important that the consumer countries think long and hard about this. Such reflection could take place under the aegis of the international community, that is to say, the IMF. A free society does not function without rules. Although the international community is able to cooperate quite well on the political level, it should also be able to do so on the economic level.

CEA: *Even if what happens today in the Gulf cannot be seen as a North–South clash, do you not think, Minister, that there is some element of this there?*

PB: Do you put Iraq in the South category?

CEA: *Iraq is part of the South even though it is a rich country.*

PB: Iraq is a very rich country whose government has not solved its problems either through its military action against Iran in a ruinous conflict that lasted eight years, then in a huge rearmament process. Iraq cannot be considered, nor can Saudi Arabia, as a Third World country. They are very rich countries. And it is obvious that when there is a rise in the price of oil because of the needs of military financing in the region, the first victims are not the industrialized countries of the North but the non-oil producing countries in the South.

CEA: *What significance has a new international order in the Middle East for France?*

PB: In that region of the world we can see what the problems are and therefore know what should be on the agenda at international conferences. The first is the Arab–Israeli conflict. Contrary to his intentions, Saddam Hussein did not manage to drag Israel into the war. He tried to do it in such a way as to create a feeling of anti-Zionism inside the Arab world. Wisdom prevailed in Israel, and I am very pleased that it did. Nevertheless, the Arab–Israeli conflict has not gone away. And Israel must make peace with its neighbours. Israel must live in safe and recognized borders, in accordance with United Nations resolutions. Also the Palestinians must have a homeland, a country in which they can build a state. It is not an easy subject, and has been unsolved for half a century. Nevertheless, we must solve it. And the problem cannot be overcome through the destruction of Israel, nor through ignoring the reality of the Palestinian problem. The second problem is that in such a heavily-armed region there needs to be some form of gradual disarmament, and at least control of the arms that there are already. The spread of nuclear capability, like that of biological weapons would severely threaten peace in the region, and doubtless beyond the region. The third issue, which I have already referred to, is that of economic development. We must organize the distribution of wealth better, and encourage proper cooperation between the industrial nations concerning overpopulated countries which do not have raw materials, and proper reflection upon the appropriate economic and agricultural development of these countries. These three sets of problems should be tackled through a proper dialogue between the countries and the governments concerned with the help of the international community.

CEA: *France is not only preoccupied by what is happening in the Gulf but also among the Arab countries of the Mediterranean region. And yet France's attitude seems to be little understood on the other side of the Mediterranean. What are your views on this?*

PB: My first reaction is that it is quite understandable for the Maghreb countries to disagree with France on given issues; they are independent countries and it is not our place to tell them what their views should be. And they should not tell us what our views should be. And I hope that with the end of the Gulf War reason will prevail over passion. The demonstrations that have taken place in these countries should be analysed with great care. There is no doubt that among certain groups of the population there is real support for Saddam Hussein. The Arabs have for a long time, as far back as the crusades, in fact, had an acute feeling of humiliation, and of not having played their proper historical role. Colonialism also contributed to this view, although France did bring some improvements in spite of its unawareness of the deeper cultural and historical realities of these countries.

Secondly, some of the demonstrations were aimed at the status quo in their own countries, even against their own governments. What is true, is that we must begin to see the question of the development of the Maghreb countries in new terms. We have made a very significant effort vis-à-vis those countries, whether in terms of bilateral aide to Morocco and Tunisia, help with the balance of payments in Algeria, a petrol and gas contract advantageous to Algeria, signed in 1982 after Mitterrand's gaining the French presidency, and so on. I would add that we also provide significant aid to those countries in the form of large scale North African immigration into France. This is a significant source of income for these countries. Sometimes this creates difficulties for us in France, but the responsible attitude of the Maghreb community in France throughout this difficult period has been extremely reassuring. Each community realised that it must respect the other without expressing their view in such a way as to give great offence, and which would have jeopardised relations between the two communities.

Economic development in the Maghreb will have very positive effects upon the world economy, on condition that the areas of financing investment are found, and that there is an increase in savings throughout the world. From this point of view the reduction in interest rates could be of help, assuming the reduction is not limited to the United States.

CEA: *What is the future of Europe in the world context, given that today the world is dominated by the United States?*

PB: Let me put your question another way; why is it that the US exercises such dominance? The answer is because of the collapse of the Soviet Empire. But the United Nations have also found ways of reaching agreement between themselves. You will say that the US was the dominant factor here too, and significantly so in terms of presence in the Gulf region. They were, however, mandated by the UN. So it depends to a certain extent upon our own political will to make the US—for which I have a great deal of respect; it is after all a democratic country, which is not the case for Iraq—act with us and with others within the framework of the UN. We need to get away from simplistic categories. The decision to apply the UN resolution, after the passing of the deadline, was taken by the US Senate by 52 votes to 47 after a debate that lasted three days. The decision could have been a different one. In France, too, Parliament supported the decision and the majority supporting President Mitterrand was even greater. What I mean by this is that democracy is a great strength for the international community, because it gives time for reflection and it stops one man, whoever he may be, from deciding issues that affect everyone.

To sum up, we must be practical. The collapse of the Soviet economy means that Russia will not play a significant role in the near future; Japan, which has become a great economic power, has still not become a great power in political terms; Europe as an entity was not indifferent to events in the Gulf, but with the exception of the two victors of the Second World War, Britain and France, Europe was unable to demonstrate a common military view; and that in spite of the fact that the Europe of the Twelve is the greatest economic and commercial power in the world. The lesson to be drawn from this, and which is the French President's and the French government's view, is that economic and monetary union must be developed further, and developed in parallel with political union in the aftermath of the Gulf War.

French Intellectuals and Arab Nationalism

Rudolf El Kareh*

Since 2 August, 1990, the conflict in the Gulf—which is first and foremost a *political* crisis—has gradually undergone a transformation. In its regional context, the Gulf conflict should be seen as the latest manifestation of a process which since the end of the Second World War and above all since the 1970s (particularly after the demise of Nasserism) has linked the major 'allies or adversaries' of the Middle East in a common ambition— to convert their power into regional domination. In the sense, the Gulf crisis is in essence part of a struggle for hegemony. Since the invasion of Lebanon by the Israelis, Israel, Iran, and Iraq have been the most important actors in this power play but in certain specific ways, so too has Saudi Arabia.

The autonomy of each of these actors has only been relative. Their flexibility and margins for manoeuvre have been dictated by the balance, but more importantly by the 'imbalance' of power between the two superpowers. A one-dimensional analysis of this new phase in the Gulf crises—of which the war has only been the latest stage—would dismiss it as an aberrant event. However, the real and manifold significance of the war must be sought in the complex interaction of many elements linked to the local, regional, and international situation.

The character of the conflict, and especially the intellectual commotion which has accompanied it—stirred up daily by the

* Professor of political science at the *Institut d'Etudes Politiques* in Aix-en-Provence, France.

newspaper and broadcasting media—would seem to rule out a dispassionate analysis. But is it really the case that critical reason has to be driven out of the intellectual debate by the military logic and 'operational Manichaeism' of the conflict? Or that intellectuals should be reduced to their organic function of providing legitimation for the choices made by decision-makers?

The circumstances have in fact made a genuine debate difficult and have opened the way for all sorts of scandalous mis-interpretations and falsifications of Middle-Eastern history. The point of this article is not to make an inventory of these infringements of intellectual integrity but rather to cast some light on one of the most important, found everywhere in the mainstream of commentary on the crisis: the systematic attempt to delegitimize Arab nationalism. This assumption that Arab nationalism is not legitimate sets itself up as being beyond the ideological debate and as a 'moral' discourse whose objective is to stamp opprobrium and ignominy on all those suspected of opposing the dominant 'Manichaeism'.

Disinformation is an aberrant phenomenon, but it does have its own internal logic. The first floodgate of disinformation was opened by George Bush and Margaret Thatcher who quickly likened Saddam Hussein to Hitler, the symbol of this century's 'absolute evil'—Nazism. The syllogism; Saddam = annexation, and annexation = Aschluss, thus Saddam = Hitler, is put forward to justify the comparison, but historically the argument does not stand up for at least one reason: the Anschluss was met with the enthusiasm of the overwhelming majority of Austrians, while in Kuwait, Saddam Hussein could not find one Kuwaiti, even in the opposition to the régime, to constitute a puppet government. Henceforth, a posteriori, the political objective of the 'hitlerian diabolization' of Saddam Hussein was transparently clear. The 'Anglo-American' war aim (to use the expression of the English language press) was to totally destroy Iraq and to force a surrender on Saddam Hussein like that imposed on his German counterpart in 1945, regardless of the incom-mensurability of Iraq and Second World War Germany. The accuracy of the comparison mattered little though. What was important were the consequences, the need, that is, to eradicate the evil through the systematic destruction of the country's infrastructure, and the elimination of both its political system and its 'Nazi' leaders. The cult of personality prevailing in Baghdad made the manipulation of public opinion—massaged daily by the incessant flow of televised images—that much easier. Curiously, the totalitarian dictators of the Eastern countries or the 'genial Kim Il Sung' had never been compared with Hitler. Why? After all, most of these dictators, and many others besides, have little to distinguish them from Saddam. First, there is the argument which claims that some dictators are less bad than others, not because they are, but because they have made the right choice of alliance, in rallying to the 'forces of good'. This reasoning has been used for sometime with regard to Latin-America and the Far East. It is now being used to define foreign policy in the crisis in the Gulf.

But this explanation is partial. The Anglo-American political objectives have also been given explicit intellectual support in a much more complex and insidious way.

First, many intellectuals who have played the role of 'organic intellectuals' in the Gulf crisis, have provided objective jus-tification for the political choices made (and even, after a certain point, have justified them in advance) in a fit of bellicose fervour which revealed above all their profound ignorance of history and their under-estimation of the impact of a war which one day would have to be concluded with a peace settlement.* Thus, in the most simplistic of interpretations (which often reduced the Gulf crisis to an arithmetical analysis of military technology) the real historical reasons for the crisis were hidden. Analysis became subordinated to a sort of Euclidean demonstration of military geometry, based on the following assumption: that the régime was equivalent to the population plus its 'Führer'. A cultural—and statist—vision of history dominated this interpretation. Thus the 'violence' manifested in the political life of the country was not seen as the product of its political history but was

---

* Cf. Hannah Arendt, *The Origins of Totalitarianism* (Unwin, London, 1958).

depicted as an element of the 'Iraqi nature'. Thus, the 'violence' used as a political weapon in the region since the beginning of the century was transformed into a type of *cultural destiny*. What an effective smokescreen to cover up the responsibility of the European powers, and notably the British, for sowing the seeds of regional political instability at the beginning of the century.

It was also easy for the British to forget, amidst the imagery of the 'Saddam = Hitler' equation, the massive use of gas by themselves in quelling the Iraqi insurrection of 1920 in which several thousand died. Certain 'Arab intellectuals' too have become the professionals of selective amnesia.*

Intellectually comfortable, because it is based on the difference between 'them and us', this approach is also related to a perverse and ideologically based conception of 'Arab nationalism'. This is manifest in the exclusive reference to the 'Hitlerian model'; all nationalism being basically 'Hitlerian in essence', 'Arab nationalism' is therefore Hitlerian. By adding up the negatives it then becomes simple to produce the 'image' desired. Hans Magnus Enzensberger used this technique in 'Adolf Hitler reincarnated' and thereby secured himself an honorary place in the history of analogical reasoning:†

To compare Saddam with Hitler is to reveal the destructive and ultimately suicidal nature of the final shape of nationalism, in the North as in the South [...] The new enemy of humanity is behaving no differently from his predecessor. [...] We are not dealing here with either an Arabic or a German phenomenon, but with an anthropological phenomenon.

There follows an argument which aims to explain that the circumstances which allow an 'enemy of humanity' to emerge are that 'he is able to find partisans who believe they are fighting against the decline of their society and that there is a sense of a long enduring sickness in the social body which has undermined

* Alain Finkelkraut in the French television programme '*le poing sur la table*' of 14 February, 1991 (TFI).
† *Libération*, 11 February, 1991, p. 16.

the self-confidence of millions of men'. Enzensberger lumps together 'German and anti-capitalist, blood and soil, anti-colonial, pan-Arab and Islamic nationalist sentiments.

One can understand the terror expressed by Enzensberger in the face of the crudest and most brutal forms of ascendant nationalist extremism. One can only marvel, however, at his ignorance of what he discusses with such aplomb. Firstly, and quite differently from Hitler, Saddam Hussein has never described himself in these nationalistic terms. Second, Arab nationalism has never been of the 'blood and soil' variety—we will return to this point. Finally, on what authority does the author characterize Iraqi society as a sick social body? With regard to its 'sociological modernity', and in terms of the dynamic development of its social body and even the norms of modernity defined by the criteria of industrial society, the progressive urbanization of Iraq over the last few decades, and its capacity for integration and technological development provides evidence to the contrary. It could be objected that this potential has been directed towards military objectives. Certainly. But who would deny that the dominant models of 'the path to modernity' as presented by the industrial societies, and above all the United States, are based on the formidable mythology of the mastery of military technology: SDI or 'Star Wars' is only the latest manifestation. Should the modernity—albeit factitious—of Brazilian or Israeli society be defined by their ability to master nuclear and ballistic technology and tanks or the manufacture of washing machines?

Of course, from the point of view of a universalistic humanism, all 'nationalisms' are execrable due to their restrictive and negative definition of their own mythical, symbolic and/or real nature in relation to humanity. But this argument must be pursued to its logical conclusion. It must have the courage to affirm, as did Professor Yeshaiyahou Leibovitz, using the terms of the Austrian philosopher Franz Grillparzer: that the path of nationalism is one 'which leads the people of humanity from nationality to bestiality [...] from the moment that one reduces human values to those of the nation, state or fatherland, or to those which derive from them, Man becomes a cruel beast'.* It must also have the courage to denounce in a non-selective way the consequences of the rise of nationalist extremism and all nationalisms. In fact, double standards abound. Nationalism is an inescapable characteristic of the world in which we live. There is no logic which can justify some nationalisms but not others. I should stress that here I am referring to the nation and national sentiment as a sociological and historical phenomenon and not as the path followed to its end—that of bestiality—by the German people, as Professor Leibovitz describes it. In other words, how can we possibly accept something in France which we denounce beyond its borders? That, however, is exactly the reasoning of all those who support the toughest treatment of 'Saddam Hussein' and Iraq. Increasing, in the discourse of those warmongers for whom 'the war is a necessary one',† the former is being used as the justification for destroying the latter: 'the war prosecuted *against Iraq* by the international coalition is necessary and just, and must be pursued to its logical conclusion [...] the victory against Iraq'. And *not* the victory of 'international law'—the recognized regulator of relations between states, and the only legitimate basis for United Nations action—albeit, as Perez de Cuellar has remarked, a rather unstable one.

For what is Iraq guilty of exactly, beyond the misguided and brutal methods employed by Saddam Hussein? Of having violated the principle of the sovereignty of states recognized by the United Nations? Certainly, but the crime would have been less— as the new warmongers should remember—if Baghdad had not called for a regional redistribution of oil income: 'the war is necessary from a political, strategic, and economic point of view' (and the fact that the region produces 40% of world oil resources makes intervention even more essential). The 'organic intellectuals' have been effectively employed.

* Extract from a conversation filmed with the Israeli film maker Eyal Sivan published in the *Revue d'Etudes Palestiniennes* (no. 37, Autumn 1990, pp. 89–99) and used in the film '*Izkor, les esclaves de la mémoire*' prize winner at the *Festival International des Programmes Audiovisuels* (1991) in Cannes.

† A. Finkelkraut, A. Touraine, and others (cf. *Libération* 21 February, 1991, p. 12).

Firstly, we had the discourse of the politicians. Hitler is not the only 'parallel'. Two regional 'precedents' have also been exhumed and disconnected from their historical contexts: Nasser and Mossadegh. Of course, the fact that the history of Nasser or the short-lived desire of the Iranian leader for independence cannot be divorced from a context of national liberation and decolonization in which those élites who fought for independence were part of a growing movement which had not yet been perverted by authoritarianism or side-tracked by ideology, is conveniently ignored. What is important is the *symbolic* use of comparison. 'This desire for expansion by a dictator—and the disregard for law and treaties—revives some old memories: those of Hitler and pan-Germanism, as well as those of Stalin who resurrected for his own purposes the pan-Slavic aspirations of the Tsars'. These words were spoken on the 23 October, 1956 by Guy Mollet. George Bush and Margaret Thatcher have hardly been original.

In the second phase the discourse was given intellectual legitimation. For those intellectuals who have taken it upon themselves to provide legitimacy for this war, the occasion to take a swipe at what they consider to be the ideology at the origin of all these evils—Arab nationalism—is too good to be passed up. Any weapon will do, including omissions, false comparisons, and theoretical hotch-potches. The occasion is ideal for demonstrating that the Arab world has never existed except in the distorted ideas for some ideologies and to this the origins of Arab nationalism must be discredited. It is not sufficient simply to assimilate them to Nazism—the absolute evil. Its very essence must be shown to be perverted. There is no hesitation to engage in deception, and reasoning by analogy has worked wonderfully, despite the fact that it is basically infantile. the arithmetic of syllogistic equations has been widely used: Baathism is assimilated with Arab nationalism, yet its 'Nazi inspirations' are also emphasized. But where, in which texts, on what historical facts are these assertions based? No one knows! But it doesn't really matter because what counts above all is anathema and ex-communication.

Thus, analogy has bordered on conflation, and shameless deception has become common. The 'Baath', the party of the 'Arab renaissance' whose objective is 'unity, liberation, and socialism' has been characterized as a 'national socialist sect'. This totally ignores its real history and origins, its ideology as expressed in the writings of its founders, Michael Aflak and Salah Bitar. 'Arab unity', say the latter, 'is an ideal and a model. It is the new idea which must accompany, inspire and drive forward the struggle of the Arab people to gain freedom and achieve socialism [...]. The Baath is a nationalist movement which is directed at all Arabs, all religions and all sects, supports the freedom of belief and treats all religions with equal respect and estime.' The project is Arab unity based on historical, cultural, and linguistic heterogeneity. Nowhere do we find in this ideology the idea of 'biological purity' or the racial supremacy of Nazism, which inspired, for example, the 'Syrian National Socialist Party' of Antun Saadé where one does find the idea of a nationalism of 'blood and soil' in the 'Fertile Crescent'. (That party, by the way, was often the tool of the British.) When founding texts are ignored and the ideals of the Baath are ideologically distorted, analogies can operate smoothly by making reference to the Nazi model:* 'The Baathist ideology contains the seeds of racism which are now easily perceived in the Iraqi Baath party' (where? how?—it doesn't matter because the inquisitorial approach is based on anathema rather than reason).

The assimilation of Baathism and European fascism is not surprising. Both are secular, irreligious ideologies (although 'secular' is frequently conflated with 'pagan'); and it is true that the Baathist forces of Syria and Iraq have killed thousands of their 'Muslim brothers', Shi'ite opponents, and Communists. But to identify Baathism with Nazism amounts to a gross misrepresentation of the facts. But that was how Michael

* Once again, selective amnesia is rampant. Since 1970 and the changes which have occurred in Baghdad and Damascus, 'Middle East specialists' have learnedly explained to us how the Baathist ideology has fallen into disrepute. To believe the 'new Islam specialists', Islam effectively buried Arab nationalism six feet under.

Tibon-Cornillot presented Baathism on 14 August, 1990 (in the newspaper *Libération*). And he added, 'We now know better how the process of "displacement" operates, in which symbolic religious structures which separate the elected from the rest continue to feed the nationalist imagination. They are most often expressed in the form of biological ideologies, allowing a hierarchy of humanity to be constructed and the inferior castes to be brutally treated. It is *undoubtedly here* [emphasis added] that we must seek the reasons for the barbaric treatment of the Kurds and for the cynical contempt which underpins aggression against the Iranians.' The massacre of the Kurds and the launching of a war against Iran are unjustifiable crimes. But this does not authorise Tibon-Cornillot to contradict historical facts.

'Baathist ideology' has become a crude explanation for the gassing of the Kurds at Halabja by the Iraqi régime in 1989, and the distortion of Baathism allows a distortion of the real historical facts. But the 'excommunicator' cares little about that. He never refers to the fact that after the Baathist *coup d'état* in July 1968, at a time when the 'Baathist ideology' was still a political motor force—and not yet an a posteriori legitimizing discourse—the government in Baghdad recognized on 11 March, 1970 the national existence of the Kurds, and their right to use their own language and administer their own region after negotiations with the Mullah Barzani. That doesn't sound like a 'fascist, racist and totalitarian ideology'! A report published by the CIA in 1974 showed that Barzani broke the agreement at the request of Iran and the United States. Nor does he mention that there has never been any reference to any 'biological unity' of the Arab nation, still less to a 'chosen people'. And there is never any reference to the fact that Baathism is an ideological hotch-potch, and that its socialist aspirations are very vague, and limited largely to a desire to see the state play a dominant role in giving cohesion to the segmented societies inherited from the Ottoman Empire and the Franco-British mandates. Nor to the fact that several ideological Baathist texts are full of references to democratic pluralism and the organization of free elections. Does an 'objective researcher' not have a duty to consider why an ideology should gradually become perverted when the state apparatuses of Baghdad and Damascus have been constructed by fragmented social forces, linked by alliances of interest and complex networks of class?

Finally, we would never know from recent commentary that through its rejection of 'confessional communitarianism' Baathist ideology is anything but 'a vision of a biological hierarchy' of human categories. In fact it is this sort of totalitarian and neo-fascist vision which has prevailed, for example, in the dominant interpretation of the Lebanese civil war among the majority of 'intellectuals' and in French and European policies (the 'Maronites', 'Sunnites', 'Shi'ites', etc.). It amounts to an identification of individuals with the only thing over which they have no power: the place and context of their birth, conceptualized principally in political terms. Have we not seen, at the worst moments of the Lebanese conflict, the appearances of 'university theses' which, under the influence of the most dubious form of socio-biology, seek to prove the 'genetic differences' between the communities in the Lebanon? Also we have seen no reference to the fact that one of the first political acts of the 'Baath' was to eradicate the confessional division of seats in the Syrian parliament because the division was inherited from the period of the mandate. The deceptive intellectual discourse clearly has its objectives. It is not only aesthetic. By conflating Saddam Hussein with the Baath, it seeks in effect, by a sort of 'spiritual linkage' to delegitimize 'Arab nationalism' since the Baath is one of its components.

The reductionism of analogical reason creates a sort of 'cocktail' of misinterpretation. In attacking the Baath it is primarily the 'Arab' element of this ideology which is the target. Once again, this is hardly new. In the past, Emmanuel Berl* spoke of the 'new Hitler' when discussing Nasser and assimilated his Arab nationalist ideology with that of the 'Arab nation'. Divorced from their history, content, and spirit, words and ideas become the stuff of fantasy. 'Pan-Arabism' is thus equated with

* Emmanuel Berl, *Nasser tel qu' on le loue.*

'pan-Germanism'. But since pan-Arabist ideas are also tainted with socialism, the linguistic conflation of 'national' with 'socialism' quickly produces the term 'national-socialism' to describe the Arab national movement. To liven up the 'cocktail', the 'anti-Zionist' nature of the Arab liberal movement, notably after the creation of Israel, adds the final, essential ingredient since Arab anti-Zionism (which is *primarily* a rejection of the antagonistic position taken by the 'Jewish national movement' towards the Arab and Palestinian national movement) is equated with anti-semitism. Thus all the ingredients have been added to this potent cocktail. Through this cunning and deceptive assimilation of Arab nationalism with the absolute evil (Nazism) there seems to be a deliberate attempt to use anathema to overshadow a fundamental question: can there be double standards in allowing movements to believe in national utopias? For if 'Jewish nationalism' (as embodied in the Zionist movement) is allowed its utopian aspirations, why is 'Arab nationalism' banned and pilloried for its own national beliefs?

As for the idea of 'humiliation'—which has been put forward to explain the identification of the Arab people with Saddam Hussein—a more detailed analysis is required. 'Humiliation' is simply a profound feeling of anger against injustice and the treachery of the colonial powers at the beginning of the century: against the breach of trust with Faisal of Arabia and the duplicity of Balfour and Sykes-Picot, against the perpetuation of a distorted and unequal system of oil income distribution, against the double standards in the treatment of the Jewish national movement and its state and the Palestinian national movement, against the obstacles placed in the way of industrial progress in the Arab countries whose citizens have only had the right to consumer (rather than producer) status, and against the protection given to the worst of dictators and despots so long as they conform with the designs of the great protectors; when they do not they are vilified and destroyed.

Finally, it is the case, although never mentioned by the 'organic intellectual', that Arab nationalism has its origins in the period *preceding* the tumultuous events of the twentieth century in the region. To mention this would totally undermine the foundation of the analogical reasoning which these days seems to pass for thought. For the origins and values of Arab nationalism cannot be divorced from the history of European ideas in the nineteenth and twentieth centuries, and it is therefore impossible to understand one without reference to the other. The cultural Arab renaissance of the nineteenth century went hand in hand with a rejection of ethnic or racial sectarianism and aspired to transcend religious affiliations and create a true secular state. Arabism thus sought to identify a common heritage, undivided by religion and faith. A common culture, language and project which would provide the pillars of a modern society. For this reason, Arab nationalism cannot be reduced to the Islamic 'Oumma', the 'community of believers' as certain of the new psycho-analysts (like Daniel Sibony) of the 'Arab-Islamic soul and subconscious' would have us believe. These people seek to probe the innermost depths of the Arab 'motherland' without considering before they start whether in fact the territory they are seeking to explore is not the product of their own imagination and of the false equation of the Arab identity with Islam. Furthermore, following one of the Arab thinkers most ignored by the new Islamic specialists who are obsessed with the 'Islamic', Sateh el Hossari, Arab nationalism railed against 'pan-Islamicism' in all its forms. The reasons are obvious. Arab nationalism—as a pragmatic programme—rejects the idea of the Arab national unity based on ethnic-racial foundations, as well as links with organized religion; for Arab civilization preceded Islam and Jews and Christians were profoundly associated with it. Above all else, El-Hossari conceives of Arab developments in terms of a dynamic in which the community of language and civilization generates a movement which is constantly evolving and which engages the participation and responsibility of all those who feel committed to a common destiny. The focal point of Arab nationalism is not located in some mythical past, in a golden age which the Islamicists hold dear; but in a process of culture development in which the Arab societies, associated in a community and with a common destiny, can be the makers of their own history.

Thus, the perverted metamorphosis of a sectarian and ideological régime is used, by association, to attack the very idea of modernity in the Arab world. The objectives of this attack are many, but the combination of contradictory elements in the attempted excommunication of Arab nationalism should not surprise us.

Since modernity is identified with the industrial 'West' and as Israel constitutes the 'regional model par excellence', access to modernity is equated with alignment with Israel. The delegitimization of Arab nationalism is a useful occasion also to bury the idea of an autonomous Arab modernity, achieved voluntarily and by the active involvement of the Arab societies in the context of a genuine democratic process.

For the new 'specialists of Islam' the delegitimization of Arab nationalism is essential. It would allow the final victory of an intellectual process which, having begun more than twenty years ago, and driven by a 'fascination with Islam', has systematically discredited all the currents of Arab nationalist thought. The encirclement of the Arab nationalist movement by the 'Muslim periphery'—the objective of the Wahhabite attack on Nasser—has found new strength in the war in the Gulf. The assimilation of the 'failure of Saddam' with that of Arab nationalism will help legitimize the accession to power of totalitarian Islamic movements, which numerous strategies are currently seeking to achieve. It will also help to redefine political 'strategies' based on an arbitrary geo-political division of an actual shared historical space around the Mediterranean; the idea of a 'western Mediterranean' is the first sign of this.

The Utopia of European union will make no historical sense south of the Mediterranean if, in turn, it does not recognize the validity of the Utopia of Arab union. The security of the societies on the northern flank of the Mediterranean will remain illusory if the societies of the southern flank remain historically and culturally emasculated.

The Twenty-first Century Has Arrived

*Didier Motchane**

The twentieth century was the keenly-awaited offspring of an ailing era; yet its own fate has been to have orchestrated its own untimely end. Extinguished by war, it has terminated, like its predecessor, in a defeat for Europe. Such an abrupt end to our century may well have been inevitable; what is certain, is that the Gulf war has been the first truly successful international policing operation in history (apart from Marshal Waldersee's successful campaign during the Boxer rebellion in China in 1900). But it will have scarcely altered attitudes within our democracies at all: we are unmoved by the world's anguish unless directly threatened; and the Gulf war, which killed only two hundred or so people, can hardly be called a war at all. Unless, of course, we include the hundreds of thousands of civilian and military Iraqi deaths: but they cannot be accurately counted—and don't count anyway. To compare the Gulf war—a six-week long military battle with Iraq by official representatives of international law and world order, or even the Second World war: Nazi butchery, the division of the world into two camps; the enslavement of Europe; promises of renewal (subsequently to be crushed by the Cold War); the impotence of the United Nations and the half-fulfilled promises of emancipation for so many peoples—with the inaugural war of this century, waged to replace the waltz with the Charleston and to rid Europe of an internecine concert of nations in favour of the League of Nations and an illusory system of collective security. What is true is that both the Great War and the Gulf War shattered certain illusions and created still more; and that, in the space of a century, we have

---

* Member of the Directing Committee of the French Socialist Party.

137

just progressed from one form of capitalism, imperialism, and colonialism to another.

During the twentieth century, revolutions came to their term, Socialism exhausted itself, the exotic became mundane; Stalin built his gulags. Surely we should feel relieved to have broken with history and to immerse ourselves in Fukuyama's super-market and mail-store catalogue ideology? Politics is politics now; war is just war. The Berlin wall took the twentieth century with it when it fell, and Baghdad gave us both its successor— the post divided Europe, post-Yalta age—and its successor's very own first world crisis. Destiny has still to decide on the final outcome of the Gulf war which, consequently, cannot provide us with a definitive vision of our 'new' history; but the possible scenarios that it does depict clearly exclude glossy visions such as those proposed by Bush, Mitterrand, or Hussein himself. The Gulf war was not about international law, the United nations, Muslims, Arabs, or Europe; it was about the United States. Arabs will now find that their internal divisions, their destitution and illusions are greater—and more bitter—than ever; Palestinians and Israelis will see that History has locked them into an increasingly desperate confrontation, and the hard-won ties established by peoples on either side of the Mediterranean have been sentenced to an early, untimely grave; Europe, finally, has been reduced to a state of near-fatal submission.

What the sheer speed of the Gulf military operation did was to blind public opinion, at least to begin with, to the real consequences of the war. For in acclaiming Bush *et al.* the 'winners' of the war, the public's mind was far removed from the likely outcome of the fine intentions, speeches, and gestures of these statesmen. There is a simple way to judge this outcome: will the war—yes or no—have helped to further world peace, justice, solidarity, and understanding?

The United Nations vs. the United States in the new world order

To a certain extent, the Gulf was *was* about international law and order; or rather, it had the potential to be. But what actually happened was that the United States was far too hungry for power, the Soviet Union too preoccupied with its internal conflicts, China too devious, and France and the rest of Europe simply too disorganized and cowardly to give the United Nations the space it needed to build on the opportunity created by the disintegration of the Soviet Union—and so of the Cold War order—to develop the role initially drawn up for it: ensuring the intervention of international law in the regulation of conflict and in the balance of power between countries engaged in conflict. Forcing Iraq to withdraw from Kuwait could have been the first step towards creating a new system for the diplomatic— and democratic—resolution of international disagreements: had the permanent members of the UN Security Council been able to agree over the substantive issues of the war, they would have provided the UN with the operational legitimacy it still so sorely lacks. In other words, success in forcing Iraq to evacuate Kuwait would have legitimized a new relationship between the rule of military might, on the one hand, and international law and the UN on the other, and this would have made it very difficult for the UN to subsequently renege on its commitments on the grounds that it had no legitimate basis for action. Obviously, international law has now proved infallible, although the fact that Israel, Syria, Turkey, and even the UN have been exonerated of wrongdoing in the past did not necessarily mean that Hussein would get off scot-free; even so, the proper way to deal with the shortcomings of international law would have been to have let the UN Security Council be more than just a rubber stamp, and to have allowed its General Secretariat get on with the job of interpreting and applying international law in the manner most appropriate to this particular case. Instead, Washington scuppered the diplomatic initiative put together by King Hussein of Jordan two days after Saddam Hussein invaded Kuwait, and obliged its Arab allies to agree to the presence on their territory of a US peacekeeping force, which, in view of its size, was obviously not a peacekeeping force at all. As in every case except for Resolution 678 (which, in turning the embargo of Iraq into an ultimatum for withdrawal, allowed the Allies to switch into offensive mode), the USA forced the hand of the UN by presenting it with a *fait accompli* for which the Americans then sought approval. In any case, the United States was only ever half-hearted about enforcing the sanctions, blatantly treating them as a logical and psychological step in the escalation of the conflict into war; they were, moreover, able to legitimize this perception by taking refuge in the adage that the best way to ensure peace is to prepare for war.

France both championed the embargo and voted its approval of Resolution 678. At home, the French government gave no public explanation of its role; neither was it asked to. We can only assume from this that public confidence in the French democratic process has reached such a peak that there is simply no need for further debate. The French Socialist Party opted for silence on the issue. As for Parliament, the constitution of the Fifth Republic did not give it the option to decide whether to grant emergency powers to the executive for the duration of the war; we can only speculate whether Parliament positively welcomed this constitutional constraint on its powers when it compared its limited role with the responsibilities borne by its predecessor in the late 1930s.

There was a full debate on the Gulf in the USA, centred on the decision to escalate from sanctions to war. In marked contrast to the French who hold the principles of international law in high esteem, the Americans are typically concerned with more tangible questions and issues, and this was no exception. What worried the Americans in the Gulf was that human rights were being violated in Kuwait; they were far less concerned than the French by the rights of the individual—including Iraqis—in dealing with such violations. Clearly, when Iraq invaded and then annexed Kuwait, rights—full stop—were being transgressed; and what Hussein's troops subsequently did in Kuwait was enough to persuade American public opinion that America should intervene in the affairs of another state in the name of salvation and moral superiority. Such moral self-righteousness had been notably toned down by the time that Hussein began to massacre his own Shi'ite people in Bassorah, for the very concrete reason that the US Administration then considered it in its own interest to do so, in order to deflect the possibility that Hussein would be replaced with an equally evil Iranian-type fundamentalist Muslim regime.

Both François Mitterrand and Saddam Hussein were correct in thinking that America's plan for a preventive strike against Baghdad would spark off very serious debate within the US Administration and Congress as early as August 1990: what Bush was doing when he compared Hussein to Hitler on 7 August, shortly after the invasion of Kuwait had taken place, was to give a clear indication of his intention to go to war. He then set about preparing public opinion for the inevitable by invoking a particularly convincing set of arguments—that Iraq's war machine, and most of all its potential to become a nuclear power, posed a grave danger to the stability of the whole Gulf region and, in particular, to the safety of Israel. Thus the war could be justified on the grounds alone that it would rid the region of this threat by stopping the Iraqi military threat in its tracks. Where this logic fails is that destroying Iraq's military capability in fact only makes matters worse, in that it renders Iran relatively that much stronger; in any case, the true reasons for America wanting military intervention lie elsewhere.

At the deepest—and subconscious—level was inevitably a desire to rid the United States once and for all of the Vietnam 'syndrome': exorcizing the evil of Saddam Hussein would be definitive proof of the US's clear conscience and moral rectitude. The US was also seeking re-confirmation of its own status as superpower by exercising its incontestable military supremacy in a new post-Cold war era in which Germany and Japan, thanks to their financial and technological strength, are questionably the new world powers. It must have been calculated in Washington that successful military intervention in the Gulf war would also allow the US to control the world's oil supply via its friendship with Saudi Arabia, as well as to establish a permanent military presence in the region and ensure that petro-dollars were quickly and profitably recycled in the form of contracts for American firms for the rebuilding and rearming of America's Gulf allies.

The post-Gulf war order: greater instability

More optimistic voices have suggested that the Gulf war has in fact increased the chances of finding a settlement to the various conflicts in the Middle East region, in particular to the Palestinian issue. Their argument is that a combination of two factors will prove conducive to resolving this conflict: firstly, America's authority in the Gulf has been enhanced by the protection it successfully extended to its Gulf allies during the crisis; conversely, the reputation of the PLO has been severely damaged by the unequivocal support which it rashly extended to Hussein's regime. Taken together, these developments should allow Bush to simultaneously apply pressure on Israel, the Arab Gulf states, and the Palestinians to normalize their relations, and make way for Washington to begin negotiations for the creation of a Palestinian state. What it actually comes down to is that the US believes that its military victory enables it to modify and dictate the terms of any future conflict—or settlement. This is a view that effectively overlooks the existence of a second set of factors which may well pull events in the opposite direction and undermine American control of the situation. For example, the PLO's loss of legitimacy to negotiate on behalf of the Palestinians, far from inciting Israel to being negotiating with the PLO (precisely because it is weakened) has instead pushed Israel to speak only directly to the Arab states: the Israeli government, supported both by Prime Minister Shamir's parliamentary majority and much of the Labour opposition, is further than ever from acquiescing in Bush's plan to surrender territory to the Palestinians in exchange for peace in the region. What is more, there are many ways in which Israel can resist pressure applied by others, as Syria might well seek to do in the negotiations to rewrite a Camp David-style agreement between the two countries.

The case of Israel is one illustration of how events may turn out differently from how the Americans initially imagined. Equally, neither the Muslim fundamentalists nor Iran have actually been weakened by the war; nor is it out of the question that Saddam's defeat, even though it may bring about the fall of the Baath party, will make way for the installation in Baghdad of a Shi'ite regime, possibly orchestrated from Teheran. In fact, it is highly likely that although in the short term the Gulf conflict has given breathing space to the more moderate Arab regimes in the region, the long-term effect will be to hasten their destabilization. Syria's position makes this all the more likely: in return for continuing to provide *de facto* protection for virtually the whole of the Lebanon, Syria will apply pressure on the so-called moderate Arab Gulf states to keep the Palestinian issue alive, as it is such fertile ground for the striking of compromises and deals.

Certain of President Bush's statements during the war, and Israel's 'restraint' in the face of Iraqi bombing raids on its territory, were proof that the coalition was thinking strategically about the conflict. Nevertheless, given the unholy alliance in the United States—which is now stronger than ever—between the quest for military supremacy on the one hand, and the desire to prove its missionary zeal on the other, it was never really on the cards that the American-led coalition could ever have hoped to exceed a purely military victory. Having proved that it could successfully manipulate the United Nations, the USA is hardly likely to now start taking orders from the same organization, particularly—as Mr Perez de Cuellar, Secretary-General of the UN recently pointed out—as the peace imposed by the US is not a secure one, and therefore cannot be easily enforced. In fact, given the present state of world relations, even a *pax romana* can not be guaranteed.

One of the greatest problems is the additional space that has been created for external influences to take a long-term hold on the Middle East, and the erection of still more obstacles to the process of peace in the area. In addition, the likelihood of large-scale migratory movements of people from the region has been increased. On 28 February 1990, Mr William Pfaff wrote in the *International Herald Tribune* that it was simply not possible for external powers to bring about fundamental change in the Middle East, given the depth and originality of the area's history and political culture; if anything, he concluded, the future would turn out to be very similar to, if not worse than, the past. Saddam Hussein was a Baathist dictator and self-styled champion of modern pan-arabism who, when cornered, sought salvation—in his case, the uprising of the Arab world in support for his cause—by calling for a holy war. Such a desperate and ill-fated gesture was tantamount to an admission of defeat, not just of Hussein's modernist and secular Iraq, but of the battle waged by an entire culture—that of the Muslim world—to catch up with Western history and civilization. From Ataturk to Bourguiba, Nasser to Gaddafi, the loose collection of diverse peoples known as the Arab world has traversed countless breaks and reconciliations with history, in a quest for an identity which has simply left it poised between the past and the future, shored up by temporary structures—so characteristic of a young nation-state—based on a curious mix of tribalism and internationalism. And, as in the case of the Balkan states, so recently released from the grip of the Ottoman empire, modernization in the Muslim nations came about via the army and the police, and not democracy. None of Iraq's neighbours can claim to run a regime which is any less of a police state than Iraq; and the reason that Iraq is the most fascist of them all, along with Syria, is in fact precisely because it is the most modern of them all; in other words, it has carried to its most extreme forms a 'Big Brother'-style control of its population.

Hussein's failure in his quest for a holy war does not simply confirm the shifts that have occurred in the balance of power in the region and in the world as a whole; it is also about Iraq's inability to trigger in the Arab world that which would have led to internal change; in other words, he failed to coax from the ever-changing constellation of physical force and political charisma present in the regimes of the Arab nations the right components from which to nurture a future democracy. Probably only History alone can bring that about. What is certain is that our Western democracies will play no part in such a transformation, as they prefer to lend their support to the most reactionary of the world's regimes.

The Gulf war: European incoherence

With the exception of the British, who still unconsciously believe that they can rely on the Americans to pursue, on their behalf, the process of world domination they began in the nineteenth century, the Europeans were not in favour of the war. In the words of the French president, François Mitterrand on 15 October 1990, they hoped that the trade embargo would succeed, and only subsequently discovered that economic sanctions are no effective substitute for political action and that European cooperation therefore had its limits. The most noteworthy of Europe's gestures was the declaration issued by the Council of foreign Ministers of the European Community to the effect that the twelve Community member states would refuse any meeting with Tarik Aziz, Iraq's Foreign Minister, unless Aziz also agreed to talks with the American Secretary of State, James Baker. It was inevitable that the Community should find itself unable to define an independent position *vis-à-vis* the crisis, given its lack of common political goal. Jacques Poos, Luxemburg Foreign Minister and President of the Council of Ministers from January to June 1991, put his name to a column in *le Monde* entitled 'Luxemburg: at the helm for Europe'. The truth of the matter is that each member state, including the world's third largest economic power (Germany), and two of the UN's Security Council permanent members (the UK and France), remains *individually* responsible for the decisions it took in relation to the Gulf crisis. Germany's so-called 'Eurocentric' behaviour aroused particular outrage in the United States. But this was a naive, if not disingenuous reaction, for on-one should have expected Germany to divert its attentions, at that time, from unification; nor, moreover, would any other nation have acted otherwise under the circumstances.

Had Europe existed as a coherent unit, it could doubtless have averted the war. It could also have done so if France had played a leading role in the crisis. At least we can assume that this was what Claude Cheysson (former French Foreign Minister) was thinking when he said in the newspaper the *Quotidien de Paris* on 11 March 1991 that war could have been avoided, had the President of the Republic been taken seriously when he said at the outset of the crisis that economic sanctions should be made to stick, and that absolutely no negotiations could take place with the Iraqis until they gave in and withdrew from Kuwait. Yet, continued Cheysson, this was not exactly how things turned out in the event, and who could doubt, in retrospect, that the United States wanted military action? Historians will no doubt prove that this was the case, and that the sanctions option was never intended to work in the first place. So what *were* the options open to France, and why did it agree to take part in the war effort? What are likely to be the consequences of its decision? We consider it more fruitful to address these questions than to engage in endless retrospective speculation and debate.

Firstly, we believe that if France had really meant to avoid war at all costs, François Mitterrand would not have left it so late to say what he did on 24 September 1990 to the General Assembly of the United Nations or, to put it more bluntly, he would not have waited until France had already sent its *Daguet* division out to Saudi Arabia. What prompted the speech was doubtlessly the Iraqi violation of the diplomatic immunity of the French ambassador's residence in Kuwait and was not supposed to be in any way connected to the question of economic sanctions. Nevertheless, the effect was to restrict France's options when it came to the decision to go to war. What actually took place between championing the embargo and sponsoring the ultimatum issued by the UN Security Council on 29 November 1990 (Resolution 678) is more obscure.

It is hard to shake off the feeling that from the outset of the crisis, France's policy was based on the principle that it should follow the US in whatever decisions it made, even if this entailed going to war, but that it should seek at all times—except where this would have had actual consequences—to distance itself from the American position. Other factors counted too: the developments still taking place in Europe—the unification of Germany, and the break-up of the Soviet Union, for example— certainly played a key role in shaping the process which eventually led France to renege on some of its most basic commitments by joining the UK as the USA's closest ally, as did the urge to maintain France's international standing, including its seat as permanent member on the Security Council of the UN. (This is perceived as already under threat from some of its European Community neighbours, who wish to see a permanent seat representing *all* Community members on the Security Council.) We would argue that in making choices of this kind, France has effectively turned its back on what has seemed for so long to be its historical and geographical vocation: to act as a link between the two shores of the Mediterranean and, on a larger scale, between the European and Arab worlds. In so doing, it is hard to believe that France will be compensated for this by gaining authority in the councils, committees, and other meetings on European and transatlantic affairs.

France's entry into the twenty-first century has not been auspicious; and if we probe deeper, we find that its decisions on the Gulf are the result of more fundamental factors than political choice and climate. We would like to base our conclusion on an observation recorded by the sociologist M. Wievorka in the French daily national newspaper, *Libération*, on 5 March 1991. According to Wievorka, the categories typically employed by France's intellectuals to classify French society, their own place in that society, and that of French society in the world, have broken down and have largely been replaced by more pessimistic visions of social and political life. Within this new perspective, democracy is merely a panacea, bearing no actual relationship to the forces at play in society, which itself is considered to be a vacuum, lacking in meaning, content, and actors. Anything judged alien to democracy ranks as evil obscurantism in this vision. What is more, social relations in the 1980s were considered to have consisted of little more than the coexistence of the individualism of the middle classes, and the corporatist ruthlessness displayed by the few remaining collective actors. Then came the National Front, which exploited latent popular xenophobia and the increase in community identity-building amongst immigrant groups. In their international version, categories such as these impose a world view based on rejection or concern. What the Gulf war has done is to make us rethink the meaning of concepts as basic as *nation* and *state*; it has equally opened to debate certain issues of social relevance, such as the media. but what the Gulf War has done most of all is to strip bare the processes by which we in the West have distanced ourselves from many other societies—including those of the Middle East. It now remains to be seen whether we will be able to reverse the same processes, should we wish to do so. The answer lies in our ability to rediscover a universalist definition of *nation*, and a social meaning to *democracy*.

United Kingdom Defence Policy and the Gulf War

Jolyon Howorth*

London's *Royal Institute of International Affairs* marked its seventh anniversary in October 1990 by publishing, in its journal *International Affairs*, two articles on Britain's foreign policy goals for the year 2000. By coincidence, Sir Geoffrey Howe's piece was published in the same week in which he resigned from Margaret Thatcher's cabinet. Sir Geoffrey argued, 'for the greater security and prosperity of western society, for the defence and advance of western values, wider agreement on common disciplines in Europe offer the way ahead. It is our most helpful route out of the twentieth century into the twenty-first. It is a route to which Britain, greater in Europe, is wholeheartedly committed.' George Robertson, Labour's foreign policy speaker, criticized Mrs Thatcher for her Atlanticist and imperialist tendencies; but his views mirrored Sir Geoffrey's when he insisted that 'Our principle and inescapable objective now has to be on the inside track of Europe'.

Only three months later, even though Mrs Thatcher had already left Number 10 Downing Street, Britain's foreign policy must have appeared to the rest of Europe as inspired far more by unconditional 'Atlanticism' than by any long term European commitment. London had not hesitated in aligning herself with Washington when the Gulf crisis broke, nor in vetoing President Mitterrand's last minute peace plan, proposed to the UN on 15

* Professor of French Civilization, University of Bath.

January 1990, despite the fact that the initiative had been supported by other members of the European Community. The British, according to Europe's press, were the warmongers of the allied coalition. Inevitably, reality is more complex.

Britain supports the war—without wanting it

The typical British reaction to the Gulf war was quite different from the jingoism so rife in Britain at the height of the Falklands war in 1982. Although the tabloid press—mainly the *Sun* and the *Star*—tried hard to whip up bellicose feelings, there were, in fact, precious few to be found: the British were remarkable for the sobriety with which they resigned themselves to allied action against Saddam Hussein. Furthermore, for as long as diplomatic initiatives appeared to have a chance of working, many people in Britain clung to the belief that the crisis should be resolved by peaceful means. According to the polls, between September and December 1990, those in favour of a peaceful solution—even though such an outcome would have meant Saddam Hussein emerging from the war in a stronger position than when he invaded Kuwait on 2 August—accounted for just under 40% of the population, while a fairly constant 53–54% continued to believe that war was justified in order to secure the unconditional withdrawal of Iraq from Kuwait. There was only really one significant shift in the polls: this was at the beginning of November 1990, when the Bush administration decided to switch from preparing a defensive campaign to gearing up for offensive operations. This was the moment at which support for Thatcher's cabinet (already under fire for other reasons), and for Washington's Gulf policy was at its lowest—48% and 43%, respectively. British support, in any case, was marked by both concern and a lack of enthusiasm. All the polls reported that people felt personally anguished by the war. One correspondent in the *Independent* admitted that during the crisis, he had ceased to accept invitations to social gatherings. Millions of would-be travellers registered their fear by cancelling plans for journeys by plane, train, or, even coach. Following the outbreak of war, these feelings of apprehension and worry increased, as, however, did support for military action. In mid-January, support was at 62%; by mid-February, it was 75% and, whereas support for a ceasefire and settlement by negotiation had been running at 32% before the war, the figure subsequently dropped to 20%. By the time the land offensive was launched, popular support had risen to 80% (as in France). This consensus does mask some differences of opinion along the political spectrum: by the end of February, for instance, 89% of Conservatives supported the military solution, as opposed to 64% of Labour (and 68% of women). There are three main reasons for this nevertheless relatively secure consensus.

Firstly, the vast majority of the British were convinced that Saddam Hussein had no intention of leaving Kuwait unless forcibly evicted. Even those such as Denis Healey and Edward Heath who, up until 17 January, had spoken so eloquently in favour of a peaceful solution, gradually fell silent in the face of Baghdad's intransigence. Moreover, Britain's peace movement, as was the case during the anti-Cruise missiles campaign, was more motivated by moral or humanist considerations than by geopolitical or diplomatic concerns. In short, Saddam Hussein was seen as a dangerous man who had to be put in his place; the war was a necessary evil. As the front line soldiers were keen to explain to anyone who would listen, 'It's a nasty business, but we've got a job to do. The sooner we get on with it, the sooner we can all go home!'

That the removal of Saddam Hussein from Kuwait was a job for Britons (along with others) went almost unquestioned. Here again, there are three main reasons. In general, Britain's historical and, in some ways, cultural traditions predispose it to take firm action in 'sorting out' foreign troublemakers, be they Napoleon, the Kaiser, Hitler, Nasser, Galtieri, or Hussein; one of the reasons why the UK seems less reluctant to go to war than some of its European neighbours is precisely because, since 1066, none of the UK's foreign wars have been fought on British territory. Secondly, in the particular case of Kuwait, Britain's historic role in the Gulf, coupled with its action in 1961 when it repelled a first round of Iraqi military aggression against Kuwait, meant that the job of defending the emirate in 1990–91 was seen more or less as an obligation. Finally, there was the inevitable nostalgia for Britain's role as a world power, as well as continued faith in the 'special relationship' between the UK and the United States. The 'special relationship' was vigorously promoted throughout the Thatcher decade and Thatcher's influence during the first days of the crisis, which she spent in the USA, should not be underestimated. These were the particular reasons why the British preferred to gloss over the real military and diplomatic implications of the war and accept the conflict largely as a necessary evil.

Agreement at the political level over the war also helps to explain the existence of a consensus amongst the British public. Once again, three factors are of particular relevance here. Firstly, John Major himself adopted a very measured, if not modest, style of management during the war. In marked contrast to Mrs Thatcher in 1982, he devolved much of the day-to-day running of the affair to Tom King and Douglas Hurd. Moreover, where it is hard to imagine that Mrs Thatcher would have passed up such a perfect occasion to tempt Labour into a fight, Major appears to have consciously sought a common denominator with his Labour counterpart in return for a peaceful ride in the Commons. Secondly, for Neil Kinnock, whose electoral prospects in October 1990 seemed promising, it was crucial to avoid making even the most minor of mistakes on diplomatic and military affairs, as this could well have cost him his hard-won credibility, particularly as John Major's arrival in 10 Downing Street had, in fact, triggered a steady fall in Kinnock's poll ratings. By the time the Gulf crisis broke, Neil Kinnock had spent over four years ridding the Labour party of all trace of leftwing activism and had managed to put together a respected and electorally credible team; he therefore had no choice but to present himself throughout the crisis as an alternative national leader. In fact, he carried off this task remarkably well, even to the extent of stifling dissent within his party. The third explanation for the consensus is that Britain's peace 'movement' was more preoccupied with expelling its Trotskyite activists who were seeking to politicize anti-Gulf war feelings. Such division hampered its own attempts to formulate a coherent response to the crisis.

In November 1990, John Major emerged victorious and virtually unscathed from a battle waged by others (the leadership contest). By the middle of the war, he enjoyed a popularity rating of 80%. Mrs Thatcher never polled this high, and only Winston Churchill, at the height of his popularity in 1940, was ever this popular. In resigning itself to the job to be done in Kuwait, the British public reacted very similarly to the country's political leadership. The position adopted by the UK government before and after the war, however, calls for closer examination; in particular, we need to consider Britain's strategic objectives as well as their possible consequences for Europe.

Britain's strategic goals

When the Gulf crisis erupted in August 1990, Britain's influence in the Gulf region had been steadily declining for years. She was most powerful in the period between 1921—when Britain helped to establish a constitutional monarchy in Iraq— and 1958 (the downfall of the same monarchy). What hastened Britain's withdrawal from the Middle East was Harold Wilson's decision in 1967 to surrender Britain's role 'East of Suez' (although the pain of such a reappraisal was eased somewhat by the contemporaneous discovery of North Sea oil). And, with the exception of arms contracts signed with most of the Gulf states and a largely nostalgic commercial presence in some of these countries, such as Oman, it is probably not far from the truth to say that Britain did not actually have a 'Gulf policy', at least not in the sense that the French, the Americans, or even the Soviets would understand the concept. Ousted from Iraq in favour of the French, and increasingly embroiled with Iran (diplomatic relations between the two countries were suspended in 1988 following the Rushdie affair), Britain was so distanced from Gulf affairs in 1987 that Ronald Reagan had to intervene personally to persuade Margaret Thatcher to lift the UK veto placed on the American request for European assistance in providing mine sweepers for the Middle East. In short, Britain did not, initially, consider the 1981-88 Gulf war—the most deadly war on the planet at the time—as its affair.

Nevertheless, on 2 August 1990, Britain found itself caught up in what Mitterrand called the 'logic of war' over a tiny Gulf emirate. Margaret Thatcher's decision—taken in Aspen, Colorado—to lend immediate and wholehearted support to George Bush, and in fact to encourage Bush to consider more hawkish options than may otherwise have been the case, had more to do with immediate responses and short-term tactical aims than with any longer-term strategic, global vision. Saddam Hussein's regime had begun to upset the Thatcher government from the start of 1990. First there was the hanging of Farzad Bazoft (an Iranian-born journalist living in the UK) by Baghdad for alleged spying offences, despite the British Prime Minister's having lodged an appeal for mercy with the Iraqi regime. Very shortly afterwards came the 'Iraqi Supergun' affair. This involved the murder of a Canadian ballistics engineer, Gerald Bull, on 22 March, followed by the seizure, at British customs, of eight large pipes, made in Sheffield and en route for Baghdad. Both events led Britain to suspect that Hussein was trying to build a super artillery (designed by Bull) which, according to a number of sources, would be capable of firing non-conventional warheads over a distance of several thousand kilometres. On 28 March, forty ignition devices for nuclear weapons were discovered at Heathrow airport. The verbal skirmishes that took place between Saddam and many of his neighbours—Syria, Israel, Kuwait, Egypt, and Saudi Arabia—during the following few months did not fail to further irritate both the British and American governments; so great, in fact, was the level of exasperation that when the crisis did finally erupt, London and Washington were prepared. The makings of a rapid and large-scale response were already in place.

What distinguishes the British and French responses to the outbreak of the crisis is that whereas for London and Washington, the priority was to stop Saddam Hussein in his tracks, Paris was more concerned with the strategic—diplomatic, cultural, and political—dimensions of the affair. From 2 August 1990 onwards, Britain and France sought in very different ways to juggle with the military and diplomatic aspects of the crisis. The outbreak of war on 17 January 1990 was, however, to bring the two governments considerably closer together in their attitude to the hostilities.

Both the Conservative government and the Labour party officially shared the same strategic goals for the Gulf: the implementation of Security Council Resolutions 660 to 678. But translating the provisions of Resolution 678—to reestablish peace and international security in the Gulf region—into military terms created a considerable grey area. John Major and his Cabinet adopted a rather ambiguous position. For example, unlike President Bush, Britain's leadership refused to accept the physical or even political elimination of Saddam Hussein as a war aim—although admitting that such a solution would not be entirely unwelcome. The destruction of the Iraqi war machine, on the other hand, soon became an explicit goal. Tom King, the Defence Secretary speaking on the BBC on 27 January 1991, gave a clear signal that the UK's military objectives extended well beyond Kuwait. During his speech, King emphasized the importance of destroying Iraq's offensive capability, claiming that such was a logical consequence of Resolution 678 and, moreover, that to fail to do so would be to betray the British soldiers who had fought for the Allies. This was the argument that led John Major to reject the first Soviet peace plan, London maintaining that an Iraqi withdrawal must entail the Iraqi army leaving all military hardware and chemical weapons behind in Kuwait. This position was only half-heartedly supported by Labour who, before diplomatic initiatives got underway again in February, declared that lasting peace in the Gulf region did necessarily entail reducing Saddam's offensive capability. But later on, when faced with the very real possibility of a ceasefire under the terms of which Saddam would have been able to withdraw from Kuwait with all arms and equipment intact (a 'nightmare' scenario, according to the Conservatives), the Labour party sought to distance itself from the Government. Labour's view then was that the Soviet peace initiative had its merits in that it could have led to a solution in which both Saddam and his war machine were spared. Yet this difference was of little significance when it came to Saddam Hussein's own 'peace proposals', launched between 24 and 27 February, of which Labour showed itself to be just as suspicious as the Conservatives.

On diplomatic issues too, differences emerged between the Government and the Opposition. Douglas Hurd, Foreign Secretary, engaged in intense diplomatic activity from the beginning of the war in preparation for the post-war situation. Although the British government was not prepared to rule out the destruction of the Iraqi war machine, it insisted throughout the conflict that the Iraqi state should be preserved within its present borders; there was never any question for Douglas Hurd of the coalition members imposing a political settlement—either in Iraq itself, or anywhere in the region. Even so, it is widely known that representatives of several Iraqi opposition groups, including the Shi'ite organizations, were frequently received at the Foreign Office from January onwards. In the post-war phase, London categorically denied claims that the British government intended to reestablish a military presence east of Suez, maintaining that a permanent settlement must be found within the Middle East itself.

But this position too has proved to be open to various interpretations. An important diplomatic gesture was made on 20 December 1990, when Britain agreed to lend support to the unanimously adopted Security Council Resolution 681 one section of which referred to the desirability of convening an international peace conference—when the time was right—to deal with the region's problems, and in particular with the Arab-Israeli problem. But the precise nature of the British view on this issue remained unclear until hostilities were over. Up until December 1990, the British government had consistently opposed

any suggestions of holding a peace conference on the Middle
East, as had been suggested by the French at regular intervals
since 1985. Ostensibly, the refusal was based on the belief that
any such peace conference would be doomed to failure because
of the complexity of the different issues involved. According to
London, any attempt to establish linkage between the various
problems of the Middle East would only serve to cloud each
individual issue. This was the same belief that led François
Mitterrand, when he first came to power in 1981 to favour
incremental, Camp David-style diplomacy rather than proposals
for global solutions (such as the European Community Venice
declaration of 1980). Mitterrand's subsequent shift towards the
idea of preferring a comprehensive regional peace conference
was the product of two main factors: the recognition, firstly,
that incremental diplomacy does not work and, secondly, that
the Palestinian problem lies at the heart of all the Middle East's
problems.

Douglas Hurd was careful to begin his international diplomatic
round in Paris, where he repeated that the British government
would continue to support the international peace conference
option, and that any remaining differences on this issue between
Paris and London were superficial. But these differences could
well prove to be highly significant. In the absence of any official
record of proceedings, it would seem that, in the short-term at
least, the Foreign Office intended to give priority to the question
of individual and collective security for the countries of the Gulf
region; and only intended to tackle the Palestinian question later,
most probably once the situation had evolved. To the Labour
party, this seemed a regrettable approach. Gerald Kaufman,
Shadow Foreign Secretary, moved remarkably close to the French
position in maintaining that the vulnerability of the Gulf states
is not a cause, but a consequence of the region's instability.
Labour Party policy is that the post-war order should be
determined by an international peace conference; and on the
agenda, as well as the Gulf crisis itself, should be issues such as
a Palestinian homeland, guaranteed borders for Israel, Syria, and
Jordan, the evacuation of foreign troops from the Lebanon, a

solution to the Golan Heights issue, the strict control of conventional arms, and the future of refugees. Kaufmann maintained that President Bush must make it clear to Israel that even if Israel would still prefer a state of 'security without peace, to one of peace without security', this option was no longer open. Finally, the Labour party considered that the key role in the region should be played by the United Nations, not—as the Conservatives seemed originally to prefer—by the Gulf Cooperation Council or the Arab League.

It is clear that Britain has still to set out its definitive regional foreign policy goals. It could be argued that the most appropriate context for the elaboration of such a strategy is the European Community. What are the implications of the Gulf war for European cooperation on foreign policy and defence?

The Gulf war and the future of European political cooperation on defence and security

At first glance, the implications are not good, at least when viewed from this side of the Channel. The British popular press pounced on the divisions between the Europeans over the Gulf to deride the 'cowards' who entered the battlefield with fewer troops than the British. Far worse, was that even the serious press made no attempt to spare the feelings of our various European partners. In its first weekend edition of the war, the *Independent* was quick to dismiss as 'eyewash' any future notion of a common European foreign policy. It even went as far as openly to conclude that Britain is powerful enough, and independent enough, to resist any future Franco-German proposals for a common European foreign policy. Britain may well bask for a while in national pride (and self-satisfaction) in the months following the Gulf war, but a rekindled nationalism is no substitute for common European structures in the future; nor indeed, will such sentiments slow down the creation of such structures, for the UK has already crossed the Rubicon. A number of more or less influential minority groups may well continue to maintain that civilization stops at Dover—and the Gulf war has only reinforced their convictions. But it is more than probable that they will remain a minority.

Before the Gulf war, the twelve Community member states were very much preoccupied with the question of European integration, and in particular with the pressing concern of European security. Thanks to the speed with which the crisis unravelled, the flaws in European Community thinking on the security issue—which had prevented the Twelve from formulating a common response to Saddam's action—were brutally exposed. But the need to eliminate these flaws was, if anything, accentuated.

The failure of the European Community to implement a common security policy in response to the Gulf crisis has to do with many problems which plagued the European Community long before the Gulf, and which still exist today: the lack of appropriate common institutions; divergent national perceptions of the world's problems; rivalry between former 'great' powers; disequilibrium between states with economic strength, and those with military might, and so on. But those who insisted on the need to harmonize the national foreign and security policies of the twelve member states have, in fact, been encouraged by the Gulf crisis. Although the various meetings of European Community ministers, of the West European Union (WEU), and of the military chiefs-of-staff during the crisis highlighted the inevitability of national differences in perceptions of aspects of the crisis, the discussions were equally significant in enhancing each participant's understanding of the complexity of the task facing the Intergovernmental Conference on Political Union (including a common defence and security policy)—once, that is, the political climate has cooled sufficiently to allow the Conference properly to resume its work. By far the most urgent of the issues on the Conference agenda must be the redefinition of relations between Europe and the United States and, within Europe, between the WEU, the European Community and NATO. This is all the more urgent now, given that the international order will have been profoundly altered by events in the Gulf.

There is unlikely to be an imminent renewal of East–West tension (which, in any case, would be of a markedly different order compared to that of the Cold War era); but we may expect a resurgence of unchallenged American military supremacy, or, possibly, the creation of a completely new and original role for the United Nations.

In either case, the *raison d'être* of NATO, unchallenged for forty years, is bound to be questioned. It is not that Western Europe and the United States no longer share the values that united them against Saddam Hussein; nor is it a question of a weakening of the fundamental friendship between these two branches of Western civilization. It is simply that the politics of international relations is now of a different order. Tomorrow's questions (what role for the Muslim world as a political, economic, and diplomatic—or cultural, or military—power? What Europe for the year 2000: a federation of twelve? a confederation of twenty? What to do about the North–South relationship?) are likely to reveal divergent answers on either side of the Atlantic.

Solidarity between the US and the UK on military matters (where means and ends were more or less identical) is unlikely to be repeated so readily when it comes to diplomatic affairs, where London will not wish to appear tied to US-made policy. Over the last twenty-five years—but more particularly since the Euromissiles crisis—the UK has become increasingly aware that virtually all of its interests relating to international affairs are closer to those of its European neighbours, than to those of the USA. It is a realization which, for all its inevitability, has given rise to anguished debate. Mrs Thatcher's departure has, however, made things easier in this respect. All the senior ministers who resigned from her Cabinet (Michael Heseltine, Nigel Lawson and Geoffrey Howe) did so because they differed from Thatcher over the European issue; the anti-Europeans of the Tory party— Nicholas Ridley and Norman Tebbit—have been marginalized, and the majority of those now in power are, on the whole, committed Europeans, albeit of the British variety. Even John Major appears to have thrown off the Thatcherite anti-European cloak which he had so judiciously donned to ensure his election to the party leadership. His first summit encounter with Helmut Kohl confirmed the shift.

Great Britain's role in West–West relations over the next few years will be critical. Inevitably, the direct links established between the British and American armies during the conflict, and the ease of communication that comes from sharing a common language, will, in the short term at least, act in favour of the special relationship. But this does not necessarily exclude an improvement in, for example, Franco-American relations, successful experience of cooperation in battle having possibly persuaded the French to see that interdependence is not necessarily the negation of the Gaullist tradition of national independence. If the experience of international cooperation provided by the Gulf war teaches both the British and the French how to handle their transatlantic relationships in a new, and changing world order, then, somewhat paradoxically, one of the most significant benefits of the Gulf war will have been its role in furthering European integration. Britain will have learned that France's deep-seated Gaullism does not necessarily rule out successful cooperation, and that Paris's affinity with Europe does not automatically signal hostility to Washington. France, on the other hand, may come to terms with the fact that the UK's readiness to support the US line on the Gulf has little to do with well thought-out, long-term political and strategic goals, and even less to do with economic or commercial interests. Both lessons would provide refreshing relief. As for Germany, it would appear that it has already assimilated the experience of the war: that its status as sovereign economic superpower brings its own duties and responsibilities.

In the wake of the Gulf war, Europe's members have more and more to say to each other. They must now learn to listen to one another, and to draw the right conclusions from their most recent shared experience. Successfully building a new world order implies defining an appropriate role for Europe; it is to be hoped that all Europeans will rise to the challenge.

Document

Labour's Policy on the Gulf Crisis

*Mike Gapes**

The war which the Labour party did not want was set in train by decisions in which an Opposition could not be involved. Once it began, Labour unequivocally supported British troops in a conflict which could in our view only end once the UN agenda had been fulfilled. The crisis broke during the holiday season and Parliamentary recess. From the very beginning, Labour emphasised the need for the British government to act to strengthen the authority of the United Nations in all its actions. Hence Labour Party policy on this crisis has throughout been based firmly on the principle: the Security Council resolutions, all the Security Council resolutions, and nothing but the Security Council resolutions.

Labour demanded the recall of Parliament in September 1990 to press for this agenda and to clarify the position of the British government. The approach of the party leadership was overwhelmingly endorsed whenever it was put to a vote in party policy making bodies. For example, the 1990 Party Conference in Blackpool on 3 October adopted a statement by the National Executive Committee which states:

> The Labour Party unreservedly condemns the Iraqi invasion and subsequent annexation of the sovereign state of Kuwait. Recognising the threat to the Middle East and world peace represented by this aggression, we strongly support the action of the United Nations as set out in Security Council Resolutions 660–666.

* Mike Gapes is Senior International Officer of the British Labour Party, and Prospective Labour Parliamentary Candidate for Ilford South.

We equally condemn the seizure and detention as hostages of foreign nationals in Kuwait and Iraq—an act which contravenes fundamental principles of international law. We call upon the Iraqi authorities to release immediately and unconditionally all foreign nationals from detention and to allow their safe passage home.

We note with deep concern that Iraqi aggression has caused a major increase in refugees in the region. We call on the British Government to continue to offer civilian aircraft for the purposes of air-lifting refugees stranded as a result of Iraqi aggression.

We also call upon the world community—particularly the most prosperous countries—to provide further substantial aid for refugees from Iraqi aggression and for those low-income nations bearing particular burdens as a result of their involvement in the imposition of strict sanctions against Iraq.

The Labour Party considers the UK government's decision to send British forces to the region as part of the multinational force, invited by Saudi Arabia and the neighbouring Gulf States—to defend them in the exercise of their rights of self defence in accordance with Article 51 of the UN Charter—to be necessary and justifiable.

The Labour Party reaffirms the statement made by the Leader of the party in the House of Commons on September 6th '. . . that if military action were taken when sanctions had been in force for only a matter of weeks or months, or when there had been no further provocation, or when there had been no further effort to achieve agreement on a mandate to attack either in the Security Council or in the Military Staff Committee, that military action could shatter the consensus that has been built', could put into jeopardy the welcome new concept of international security, make continued participation in UN action by all members of the Security Council less likely, add to distrust and alienation in the Middle East and provide a political reward for Saddam Hussein.

In common with many other Parties and organisations and with member countries of the UN, including Security Council Members, we consider that the peaceful ending of the occupation of Kuwait by means of a blockade and sanctions would be a great advance for the system of selective security and we therefore:

1. strongly urge all governments involved in the multinational force to ensure that every opportunity is given for sanctions to work and that resort to military action not related to enforcing the blockade is avoided;

2. support the freezing of all Iraqi assets in the UK, the controls on Kuwaiti assets in the UK and the complete cessation of trade with, and credit to, Iraq until the Iraqi government complies with UN Security Council Resolutions;

3. consider that the British government must ensure that no organisation

assisting Iraq with the supply of weapons, or weapons manufacturing equipment, be permitted to continue its activities;

4. endorse the efforts of the United Nations Security Council under Resolution 670 to introduce an effective air embargo on Iraq and Kuwait in pursuit of the mandatory sanctions policy.

We believe that these measures will prove to be the most effective means of denying any form of reward for Iraq's aggression, of securing that country's compliance with the resolution of the UN, of helping to achieve a satisfactory and enduring settlement of the crisis, and creating conditions for the development of new security structures to promote peace and stability to the benefit of all peoples in the region, including the Palestinian people.

The Labour Party shares the approach set out by President Gorbachev and President Bush in their statement at the Helsinki Summit specifying that their 'preference is to resolve the crisis peacefully' and that they are 'determined to see this aggression end and, if the current steps fail to end it, . . . are prepared to consider additional ones consistent with the UN Charter.'

We believe that such an attitude signifies a full understanding of the potential of sanctions, of the implications for the Middle East of this method of ending aggression and of the need to sustain and strengthen international co-operation through the United Nations. Such co-operation has had unprecedented importance in the response to this crisis and offers encouraging prospects for the achievement of a system for attaining collective security and peace in the world in a manner long sought by the Labour Party.

An alternative resolution was defeated on a card vote by a huge majority of 4,862,000 to 635,000—eight to one—and it said:

This conference totally condemns the invasion of Kuwait by Iraq as a clear act of aggression contrary to international law and the United Nations charter. Conference fully supports the economic sanctions imposed against Iraq by the United Nations Security Council and the resolution authorising the arrangements for enforcing these sanctions.

Conference shares the profound concern of the British people and the international community about the hostages in Iraq and Kuwait. They should be released immediately and unconditionally.

Conference believes that a peaceful settlement of this dispute and other outstanding issues in the region is both possible and necessary, and that the United Nations Secretary General should be authorised to urgently explore all possibilities. It is essential, if the United Nations, is to fully develop its role and enhance its authority, that it should have the full backing of governments who should act consistently in upholding the charter.

Conference therefore calls on the British government to make a clear and unequivocal statement that it will not commit British forces to offensive military operations against Iraq unless they have explicit authorisation through a resolution passed by the Security Council, under the provision of the United Nations charter, which deals with the use of force by the United Nations, and under its military command.

In January, both before and immediately after the UN deadline, there were major debates in both the Parliamentary Labour Party and the National Executive Committee. Identical resolutions were adopted by these two pillars of the Party. The statement passed by 22 votes to 3 at the National Executive Committee meeting on 30 January 1991 stated:

This National Executive Committee:
—reaffirms its previous Resolution in support of the decisions of the United Nations taken since the beginning of the crisis caused by the Iraqi invasion of Kuwait.
—regrets that the strategy of sanctions, blockade and military readiness to achieve the purposes of the United Nations was not pursued for a longer period.
—records its deep concern at the human and ecological costs of the conflict arising from the action of the Iraqi dictatorship.
—gives full backing to the British and Coalition forces being used to secure fulfilment of the United Nations Resolutions; recognises the courage shown, and the essential contribution made by merchant navy seamen and women and other non-military personnel; and commends the instruction to avoid civilian casualties whenever possible.
—considers that all diplomatic opportunities for achieving fully the objectives of the United Nations Resolutions should continue to be explored by the United Nations and its members; and welcomes the joint statement by the United States Secretary of State, James Baker, and the Soviet Foreign Minister, Alexander Bessmertnykh, that both powers agree to work jointly to end Arab/Israeli conflicts and that:
     'a cessation of hostilities' (in the Gulf) 'would be possible if Iraq would make an unequivocal commitment to withdraw from Kuwait' . . . backed . . . 'by immediate, concrete steps leading to full compliance with the Security Council resolutions'.
—considers that in all activities against Saddam Hussein's aggression, it is

essential that every effort be made to try to ensure that the post-war peace settlement is durable and does not produce continuing resentment and resulting instability, extremism and terrorism.

—considers that, when the requirements of the United Nations Resolutions, including the complete and unconditional withdrawal of Iraqi forces from Kuwait and the restoration of international peace and security in the area, are clearly complied with, the use of force should thereupon cease.

—considers that, at the cessation of hostilities following the achievement of the purposes of the United Nations Resolutions, immediate action must be taken by the UN and the international community, using political and diplomatic means:

(i) to achieve the substantial disarming of Iraq by the reduction of conventional forces and the verified and complete removal of chemical, biological and nuclear weapons and the means of making them, and the ending of regional superpower status for Iraq and for every other country in the region.

(ii) to implement the provisions of UN Resolutions 681, 242 and 338 through an international conference under the auspices of the United Nations as an essential means of achieving lasting security and justice for the countries of the region, and for the Palestinian people.

There was of course a small but vociferous minority in both the National Executive Committee and the Parliamentary Labour Party who pressed their own agenda for a unilateral ceasefire, but the numbers voting against the leadership and Party Conference policy fell within the Parliamentary Party from 57 to 33 out of the 230 Labour MP's, and although the media gave significant attention to the few critics in the Parliamentary Party, the main party approach in support of the multi-national UN authorised coalition was widely supported by the public, and Labour voters strongly endorsed the Party's position. Five junior front bench spokespersons did resign their portfolios but it should be recognised that there are some one hundred frontbenchers in the PLP. Overall the party was strongly united behind the line espoused by Neil Kinnock in the parliamentary debate on 21 January when he stated Labour's case against a unilateral ceasefire:

Of course there are some who want the fighting to stop immediately and renewed efforts then to be made for a peaceful solution. The motives are entirely understandable, especially to anyone who is part of that great majority who did not want fighting to start if it was at all avoidable. There can be no one—at least no one of any humanity—who does not recoil from the dreadful carnage; and there can be no one who does not want it mitigaated as much as possible and ended as completely and as quickly as possible.

However, we must ask whether a ceasefire would produce that result. Would it really be likely to reduce the toll of lives? The answer must be that a ceasefire could reduce the toll of lives only if there was certainty that it would definitely produce an immediate and permanent withdrawal from Kuwait and the complete laying down of arms by Saddam Hussein. It is obvious that, in the absence of such certainty, a pause in the attack on Saddam's forces and facilities would simply provide him with an opportunity to regroup, to resupply and consequently to resist even more stubbornly.

In Iraq, a ceasefire by the coalition could not fail to give substance to Saddam's propaganda and to add further to that resistance. The result would be to prolong, not to shorten, the conflict, to postpone, not to promote, the end of fighting and to increase, not to decrease, the slaughter. None of that outcome could conform to any definition of peace or peace-making. It would not fulfil the purposes of mercy, and it would not even promote post-war stability, since it has every likelihood not of mitigating the slaughter but of leading to the increase of slaughter.

Meanwhile, as the war rages, two points must fairly be made: first, Saddam Hussein shows absolutely no inclination to comply with the basic requirements of the United Nations and quit Kuwait. On the contrary, all his words are of fanatical defiance, and all his actions of military offence. Secondly, it must be said that, by withdrawing from Kuwait, Saddam could have prevented any possibility of war. Even now, he can stop the war immediately by withdrawing from Kuwait and laying down his arms. Whatever else may be said or thought about the Iraqi dictator, some things are obvious: he wilfully refused to follow a course that guaranteed no war; he does not as yet want peace, and he will not as yet allow peace. If he does, he will get peace.

It also strongly supported him when he made clear the need to consider not just war aims but also peace aims:

Peace aims must include the purpose of keeping Iraq whole and secure from outside attack after the cessation of this war. The war aims do not include the deposing of a Government or the death of a dictator, and rightly so. They are not fit objectives for the United Nations. But the peace aims must involve the substantial disarming of Iraq by the reduction of conventional forces and the verified and complete removal of chemical, biological and nuclear weapons and the means of making them. Peace aims must relate to ending regional super-power status for Iraq and for every other country in the region if they truly are peace aims. To ignore that is to ignore the fact that great disparities of military strength and conventional and non-conventional armaments are of themselves major sources of instability.

That unavoidably means that, in the wake of this war, the peace aims must be geared to the stability of the whole of the Middle East. That requires firm and dependable long-term security structures for the region, as the Prime Minister indicated. It requires freedom from the fear of invasion or attack for nations. For peoples, it requires the recognition of their identity and their right to self-determination in their own homeland. Stability in the Middle East demands, in short, collective security operated through a United Nations with the influence to achieve political resolutions to disputes and the power to deter aggression. That influence and power cannot be wielded by one nation or by a group of nations—certainly not a grouping of nations—from outside the Middle East.

In a major foreign policy speech at the Royal United Services Institute two days later Neil Kinnock expanded on the need to reinforce the peace keeping role of the United Nations, declaring notably:

The ending of the Cold War has obviously made it possible for the United Nations to begin to fulfil the function envisaged by most of its post-war creators.

Many who have long desired that achievement—and some who didn't— presumed that it would be a gradual process with some trial, some error and, hopefully, some success.

That rather sedate view changed on August 2nd with the invasion of Kuwait.

The current action in the Gulf is authorised by the United Nations as a result of the refusal of Iraq to comply with the requirement's of the United Nations. Devastating force is being used, huge resources have been committed, vast sums of money are being spent.

The United Nations must win or be forever impotent. It must therefore be upheld as the supreme instrument of collective international security.

And then, when the war is over and the will of the UN is done, the real test will begin. The UN will have to live up to its new status and achieve success in the resolution of other conflicts and tensions.

The greatest and most immediate of those is in the Middle East.

If the United Nations secures the implementation of Resolution 660—as it will—that will be a cause for relief. If it can over time gain the fulfilment of Resolution 681 and—consequently—242 and 338, it will be a cause for the world to rejoice.

The member nations and their will for international security will determine whether that is achieved. The awful sacrifice of lives and resources that has taken place and will take place must impress upon all countries the need to see that it is.

Shadow Foreign Secretary, Gerald Kaufman, enlarged on the need for a just settlement as part of a continuous peacekeeping role for the UN in an article in the *Guardian* on 6 February 1991:

Regardless of the posture of the Palestine Liberation Organisation and in spite of the Israeli's unjustified incarceration of moderate Palestinians like Sari Nusseibeh, the Palestinian issue will not go away. As Amos Oz, Israel's great novelist, put it: 'Self determination is not a declaration of good behaviour. If this was the case, three-quarters of the nations on earth should have been denied independence.'

When the war with Iraq is over, the US must give the international conference its highest priority, indicating to the Government of Israel if necessary that future US support for that country will be dependent on Israeli participation. It no longer makes sense, if it ever did, for the Shamir government to declare that it prefers security without peace to peace without security. That choice is no longer available, if it ever was. The grim message of the Scud missiles is that Israel's security depends on peace.

The agenda for the UN conference is clear: self determination for the Palestinians; resettlement of the Palestinian refugees, financed by the Gulf states; guaranteed security for Israel and her Jordanian and Syrian neighbours, including a solution to the Golan Heights problem; withdrawal of all foreign forces from Lebanon; stringent international control over arms imports into the region; active moves to remove all nonconventional weapons from the region, and prevention of any further countries gaining such capacity. The settlement should be policed not by Western forces or even by Arab and Islamic forces, but by a UN army. The Labour Party's policy review, adopted by the 1989 annual conference, stated: 'A Labour government will make British forces available to the United Nations and the Commonwealth for peacekeeping and peacemaking duties.' Other countries, such as the US, the Soviet Union, Canada, India, Australia, and of course the Arab and Islamic countries should contribute contingents.

The agenda is massive and daunting, and will be enormously difficult to achieve. That is no reason for shirking it. Indeed, the very dimensions of the agenda emphasise the supreme necessity of tackling it right away. The deaths in the war must not be in vain.

Forty-five years ago on 10 January, 1946 in London, at the first session of the United Nations General Assembly the Labour Prime Minister, Clement Attlee, said:

> . . . in times past in these islands great nobles and their retainers used to practise private war in disregard of the authority of central government. The time came when the private armies were abolished, when the rule of law was established throughout the length and breadth of the island . . .
> What has been done in Britain and in other countries on a small scale, has now to be effected throughout the whole world.

There is no better definition of international security—and no better guidance for those who seek it.

Book Reviews

Edgar Morin and the New Beginning

Sami Naïr

The new book by Edgar Morin, Gianluca Bocchi, and Mauro Ceruti is a book of introduction. In this sense, the title *Un Nouveau Commencement (A New Beginning)** is very appropriate, for the book is all about being introduced to a new way of thinking: a new era, original questions, and novel solutions. The new era is global unity, because not only social groups, homelands, nations, and regional entities but also and above all the planet itself, the earth as a centre for the lives of each and everyone, regardless of the particular place in which they live, all share a common destiny. Since the economy has become global, modern technology holds us tight in its attractive but dangerous snare, and the unlimited expansion of information conditions our reactions in a space of time which changes our very concept of time, the way we think in relation to this world must therefore also be transformed into 'world thinking', in terms of the whole and coexistence within the material world. Who better than Edgar Morin to put his finger on this new structure and attempt to take up the challenge? Morin, the author of *La Nature Humaine*, a thinker of complexity who refused the reductionist approach, a standard-bearer for concrete universalist humanism (a humanism which obeys no 'logic' of history, no mechanical or messianic determinism), offers in his *New Beginning* a masterly demonstration of the awakening of a new century and

---

* Edgar Morin, Gianluca Bocchi, Mauro Ceruti, *Un Nouveau Commencement* (Editions du Seuil, Paris, 1991).

the promises and threats it brings with it. Beneath the fundamental conflicts which the political/ideological battle and the voraciousness of the media tend to build up into a clash of civilizations, Morin shows us the unity of structures, the common central home. Take techno-science and its opposite, neglect of historicity; take development and its opposite, economic, cultural, and even emotional under-development; take democratic preaching and its absolute opposite, totalitarianism; take abstract, positivist, and aggressive rationality and its opposite, reactive, reactionary and emotional fundamentalism; take global positivism, with its destruction of nature, and its remedy, ecology and the rediscovery of the vital importance of the natural environment. Take all of these conflicts, and you will see that, in order to resolve them, it is necessary to think of them as a whole, if you want to avoid falling back into the destructive Manichaeanism which made the twentieth century one of the most creative but also one of the most devastating periods our suffering humanity has known. Of course, it is not only a question of method, it is also a philosophical standpoint, a vision of the world. This vision forms an invisible thread through Morin's book; it calls for dynamic history to be conceived from the point of view of the real emancipation of the individual. This emancipation in turn implies some deep thinking on human rights (some very fine pages here on totalitarianism and the internal contradiction which transforms its strength into weakness), on nationalism and its aggressive obsessions, on the nation-state and its now open crisis, on pacifism and its new role in a civilized world, of the power of arms (here, too, much thought has been given to the army as an army of peace), on the breakdown of empires, particularly that of the Soviet Union, and on the creation of new transnational solidarities, an area where Europe ought to be able to provide the example, based on a modern and forward-looking concept of confederalism. The concept of world thinking, democratic confederation and the Damoclean era, among others, are used in the debate opened by Morin and his co-authors to help us understand the present and act on the future. It is a subversive book, in the highest sense of the term, because it concerns the fate of all of us, in the name of the freedom of each of us.

The Arab-Islamic World at the Crossroads of History

*Etienne Butzbach**

It is not necessary to know a situation in order to hold a point of view: this sentence sums up quite aptly the position of many intellectuals, politicians, and experts who gave commentary after commentary, analysis after analysis all through the Gulf war. To put forward pertinent arguments, it is not enough to waffle brilliantly; on such a complex subject it is dangerous to venture opinions without a minimum of prior knowledge. Too often, democratic debate suffers from ill-prepared arguments. Three books are therefore helpful in casting new light on the complexities of the Orient, from which the breaking-down of barriers in Eastern Europe had distracted our attention.

'*Laïcité ou islamisme: les Arabes à l'heure du choix*'† is a collection of texts by Fouad Zakariya first published in Cairo in 1986. The philosopher cannot find words strong enough to denounce the intellectual under-development of the Arab world: a medieval mentality, the reign of ineffectual and authoritarian thought and alienation inside outdated models of thought. . . It is a devastating indictment. In the context of the failure of the great liberal and socialist ideologies, the Arab world has for the last twenty years been going through a period of decline and regression which has paved the way for a religious revival.

*General Secretary of the IEREM (Institut d'Etudes et de Recherches Europe Méditerranée), Paris.

† Editions La Découverte, Paris ('Textes à l'appui' series), 165 pp., January 1991.

But is it fair to speak of a 'reawakening of Islam'? The author is adamant in repudiating this thesis. Followers of Islamic groups are constantly increasing in numbers, but the level of theoretical debate is deteriorating. In reality, this new form of Islam is merely an 'expression of frustration, disappointment and rejection of present conditions', the outward sign of a political and cultural repositioning.

It is the natural heir to the authoritarian way of thinking embodied in the despotic regimes which emerged directly from independence. According to Zakariya, in this authoritarian mode of thought, 'all signs and causes of a problem were considered, not directly, but in relation to what had been said previously by the holy texts and scholars of recognized authority'.

'There is no better preparation for the power of turbans than the power of the jackboot.' Clerical authority replaced military force, the previous incarnation of the same authoritarian arche-type. The post-colonial state created favourable conditions for the emergence of Islamic groups. Even under Nasser, the state never renounced its Islamic roots. In the 1970s, the Arab states lent decisive moral and material help to the Islamic movement. This 'Islamicization' from above 'broke out of the narrow confines in which state power thought it could keep it'. Zakariya establishes a direct relationship between under-development and nostalgia for the past.

Today's Islamic movement is based on an ahistorical perception of the past. It creates a temporal alienation which is more serious than the spatial alienation of intellectuals living physically in their own country but intellectually in another. This temporal alienation consists of seeking conclusive answers to problems of the present in the by-gone days of the cultural heritage. 'The originality of Arab culture lies in the fact that it does not see the past as an intrinsic part of the present but as a separate and conscious entity which seeks to impose itself on the present.'

In response to this regression to the Middle Ages, Zakariya extols the virtues of secularism, a social and political as well as historical necessity. Only secularism can respect differences and the plurality of opinions, enlarge the sphere of public liberties and respect of minorities and establish a real democracy, the condition for development.

Zakariya wages this struggle for secularism in his articles by dissecting the discourse of religious propagandists. He answers the intellectual poverty of the Islamic sermons, the lack of general culture, the 'total ignorance of opposing doctrines' and 'the vertical handing-down of ready-made formulae' with a 'critical dialogue based on education and open thought'. His writings, which have been quite widely distributed, criticize the accusations of irreligiousness or conspiracy levelled at advocates of secularism. But the most important part of his reasoning is aimed at disputing the argument that secularism is a 'product of European history'. To refute this argument, he points to the universal nature of the values of rationality, critical intellect, scientific rigour and independence in relation to intellectual authority.

The European Renaissance holds lessons for the Arab world for it is only in 'putting tradition in its historical context that one can resolve the apparent contradiction between the legitimate pride which one takes in it and the necessary recognition of its obsolescence'. In the Arab world as in Europe, breaks with the past and partial renunciations are necessary in order to move on to modernity. But the relationship between Arabs and their cultural heritage has more to do with hoarding than with productive investment. In order to combine authenticity with modernity, Zakariya insists, it is necessary to liberate the thinking of the ancient authorities, take a selective look at the cultural heritage and recognize how far it is from the present. It is all too easy for followers of the Islamic movement—and for some Arab intellectuals—to take refuge in pathological criticism of the domineering ethnocentrism of the West. However, the rejection of an essentialist view of Islam can only be credible if it is accompanied by the rejection of another essentialist view, that which confuses the Occident of knowledge, rationality and secularism with the Occident of colonialism, domination and subjugation. All too often Orientalist archetypes are the mirror image of stereotyped images of the West.

But one of these images is more valid than the other, Zakariya writes. 'Orientalism, the fruit of a knowledge for power' (the West's hegemony over the East) implies at least a minimum of accuracy, whilst 'Islamo-centrism' is the product of feelings of inferiority and makes do with curtailed knowledge. Thus, Zakariya does not offer an easy way out. He calls for a veritable intellectual revolution in order to 'call into question the very image we have of ourselves'. 'The day when Westerners translate our economic, social and political studies on our countries because they are the best reference, we will be able to begin to dig the grave of Orientalism. And I don't see that happening for a while yet.'

Zakariya's lucid pessimism is echoed in Fawzy Mansour's book entitled *The Arab World: Nation State and Democracy*, first published in Cairo in 1988.* Fawzy Mansour, an Egyptian university academic, ponders why the Arab world is incapable of adapting to the modern world. But his approach is radically different from Zakariya's, although he does adopt the latter's analysis of the ahistorical nature of religious fundamentalism. The author paints a vast economic-political-historical landscape, largely inspired by the theories developed by Samir Amin who edited this collection of Mansour's writings.

Past, present, future: the 'impasse' of the Arab world is declined in all tenses. Past: spoils of war and tributes to the conqueror made the Golden Age one of great prosperity. Unearned fortune played a crucial role from the very beginnings of the Arab world. But the nature of this wealth and the need to renew it, coupled with the inability to set up a stable legal and political framework, encouraged the militarization of society. To these different factors curbing capitalist development, Mansour, like Amin, adds Islamic universalism. The chance for business to establish itself in a vast world-wide unit prevents the crystallization of nation-states on the European model. Present: the author sees two main types of process unfolding within the Arab world: rocketing oil income and the formation of a reactionary pole; the failure of post-independence revolutions. Mansour

* Zed Books, London, 1991.

describes in detail the effects of the oil boon which will throw the development of the entire Arab world off-balance and strengthen the absolutist monarchies of the Arab peninsula. As for the failed revolutions, Egypt and Algeria are seen as systems hovering between bureaucratic capitalist and liberal capitalist forms of state. In presenting these arguments, the book has the merit of reminding the reader of the importance of the economic and political effects of oil revenue, but those not entirely in agreement with the method of analysis chosen by Mansour will draw a sharp intake of breath at the logical shortcuts he occasionally takes. Thus, the discussion is cut particularly short in Mansour's last chapter, dealing with the future. His main postulate concerns the identification of the social forces which could bring about an independent strategy of development based within a united Arab framework. This only confirms the need, spelt out by Zakariya, for greater methodological and conceptual rigour.

A central problematic element evoked by Mansour is the establishment of Israel in the heart of the Arab world. Mitchell Cohen, professor of political science at New York, provides some help here by filling out the history of the transition 'from Zionist dream to Israeli reality'.* Although it was born in Europe in the era of classes and nations, Zionism is not just a reaction to a particular historical situation. The status of Jews had already changed by the end of the eighteenth century, just as modern nationalist and racist doctrines were on the rise. The 1881–1882 pogroms in Russia caused the first modern wave of emigration, whilst the spread of Hebrew expressed the assertion of a Jewish nationalist consciousness.

Political or cultural Zionism? Theodor Herzl saw his political project triumph at the first Zionist congress in 1897. But in 1907 the Zionist synthesis encouraged the simultaneous progress of political, practical and cultural activities. Its Labour orientation and the adoption of a 'constructivist' approach showed the influence of the socialist ideology of the 1920s. Gradually,

* *Class Struggle and the Jewish Nation*. Transaction Books, New York, 1985.

however, under the leadership of Ben Gurion, the Zionist
organization moved from a class analysis to the concept of the
nation. The creation of the state of Israel in 1948 marks the end
of this first phase of affirmation of national identity.

Before putting forward solutions it is necessary to take a hard
look at the size of the problems which dominate the present
landscape: the stalemate of the Arab world, the entrenchment of
Israeli society. Zakariya, Mansour and Cohen give us some
invaluable pointers.

The Three Cultures

*Gérard Duprat**

In his book, *Die drei Kulturen*† (*The three cultures*), Wolf Lepenies is concerned with the formation of sociology and its long and difficult establishment as a scientific discipline in France, Britain, and Germany. The book traces the complex and often tortuous course of this science's history since its invention by Auguste Comte, and takes the story up to the 1930s. German sociology receives special treatment, however, since the closing pages go beyond the Nazi period to discuss some of the recent debates; French sociology, on the other hand, is really only examined until the start of the twentieth century, ending with an account of the controversies surrounding the rising influence of Durkheim's ideas. Lepenies therefore uses the French, British, and German examples quite differently. Is he thus perhaps suggesting that the dispute over the 'scientific nature' of sociology (and therefore the development of sociology itself as a science, in the relatively homogeneous cultural group which the three countries in question make up) follows a sort of progression which gives each example its significance at that particular moment in history, or at that particular phase of its development? Could this argument be applied to French sociology between Comte and Tarde, and would this mean the end of its development at the beginning of the twentieth century, when Herr and Durkheim

* Professor of Political Science at the Institut d'Etudes Politiques, Strasbourg, France.

† Wolf Lepenies, *Die drei Kulturen: Soziologie zwischen Literatur und Wirtschaft* (Hanser C, Munich, 1985).

eventually pushed sociology over to support for the Republic
and socialism? Or similarly the end for British sociology, when
the Webbs leaned towards communism during the immediate
post-war period? Or for German sociology, when in the 1970s–
1980s it finally got round to settling up with itself, just at
the time when, in the same movement of thought, German
sociologists were pondering over both *the place given in reality* to
their science in universities during the Nazi period and *the function
of producer of meanings and values* which, spurred on by its
conservative wing, it assumed in the Bonn Republic under the
liberal-socialist coalition?

In fact, although these questions are certainly present (or at
least the reader is led to pose them) in Lepenies's book, this pre-
judgement should not be accepted too hastily. The book's rather
strange historical divisions are due primarily to the completely
new approach which Lepenies takes to the debate on the scientific
nature of sociology. The book's originality lies in the way it
tackles each of these examples within the same overall perspective
and goes beyond highlighting their singularity to link them in a
common experience of meaning present in all of Europe: namely,
the relationship between sociology and literature, which made
and continues to make both of these types of knowledge of
society, either simultaneously of diachronically according to the
distinctive features of each national case, rivals or competitors
at times, but objective partners most of the time.

Hence the idea of the 'three cultures': scientific, literary, and
sociological, with the latter wedged in between the first two.
Three, and not two, as custom would have it and as C. P. Snow
suggested in a famous 1956 article in the Webb's journal, which
Lepenies takes as his starting point: on the one hand the culture
developed from science ('real' science, that of experimental
physics, which for a long time has led the 'culture' of the social
and human sciences) and literary culture on the other. Lepenies
shows that this dichotomy is mistaken: by re-placing its origin
in the social and human science projects of the Enlightenment,
Lepenies's account of the history of sociology proves that it dealt
as much, if not more, with 'pure' science, right back to Buffon.

It would be simplistic to conclude from Lepenies's book that, all things considered and given its history in Europe, sociology neither has any more to say nor has any less worth, in relation to the production of meaning and values concerning our industrial, capitalist society, than literature—apart from the charms of the latter.

Neither should we be too ready to believe that this relationship was the same, despite national specificities, in the three countries concerned until the 1930s, or that sociology as a discipline suffered a crisis of identity more or less constantly and everywhere. In fact, although the reader is left in no doubt that sociologists have existed in Europe ever since Comte, Lepenies leaves room for doubt about the existence of sociology itself. There can be no doubt that Lepenies, rector of Berlin's *Wissenschaftskolleg*, writes stylishly, and he is skilful in telling the story of the intellectual and romantic friendship between Comte and Clotilde de Vaux, which he parallels with the Webbs' relationship; he knows how to capture the reader's attention by switching the debate which he sets up between Thomas Mann and Weber to Taine and the Enlightenment, then back to Eliot, Durkheim, or Tarde via Goethe. Anything but a boring history, this is a cheery novel of sociology's life, and the pedagogue is well hidden under the scholar brimming with knowledge of European culture, although he gives his opinion on the great classical debates: the German crisis in French thought, the distinctiveness of British socialism from an intellectual point of view, the famous time-lag of German history (seen as 'backwardness' in Marxist rhetoric), cultural pessimism and the ideology of sentimental values specific to this culture, the gulf in it between poetry and literature, Curtius and Agathon. One could go on forever listing examples of the knowledge and musings in this book, which would help all young Europeans to become more concerned about the details of their history and more aware that cultural Europe, with its national misunderstandings as well as the complicities of its scientific communities and its literary rivalries, can be observed in a very pleasant way from such an apparently unattractive observation post as this 'sociology' born in the nineteenth century in the woolly thoughts of Comte. In short, cultural Europe—the Europe of intellectuals and the cosmopolitan intellect—has found in sociology a good means not of overcoming its difficulties but of crossing these centuries of iron and fire which separate us from the Enlightenment. This has never been seen so clearly as in Lepenies's book.

To conclude, two more questions. Does this sociology of intellectual debate provide a suitable framework for defining the real relationship between sociologists or literary figures (or hybrids) and politics, and for assessing the influence of their work and their debates on the course of things? For that, it would be necessary to leave the charms of history and the pleasure (that of the antique expert, as Hegel said) of following it through its myriad twists and turns. Take the epilogue of *Die drei Kulturen*, relating to German sociology in the Bonn Republic: is it possible, for example, to understand the meaning of the call to dialogue made by Schelski to Böll and to grasp the significance which Lepenies attaches to it, without first taking a dull and scholarly look at the 'facts' and making an impassionate critique of scientific policies and the policy, in the strict sense of the word, pursued by the leading groups in this sociology from 1945 onwards? Would a study of the reasons why sociology became 'politicized' in a 'definitively changed political context' and was able to attract large numbers of German youth, as Lepenies notes, not itself produce meaning?

So, three cultures? In fact, Lepenies himself reveals four cultures at work in sociology; the fourth appears throughout his book, but beneath the surface: it is philosophy, as influential as the three other cultures in shaping the sociological undertaking and its national differences. Europe's specificity is not that it has 'a culture' but precisely that it has cultivated itself through the mixture of these cultures, if that word can be applied without lapsing into reductionist unitarianism.